LIVING JONATHAN'S LIFE

LIVING
*J*ONATHAN'S
LIFE

A Doctor's Descent into Darkness & Addiction

Scott M. Davis, M.D.

Health Communications, Inc.
Deerfield Beach, Florida

www.hcibooks.com

The information in this book is not intended to replace, corroborate, or be a substitute for professional medical care. Neither the author nor the publisher accept any responsibility for how you choose to use the information presented in this book, or the suitability for any individual of any of the treatments covered.

Specific program descriptions and/or treatment information is subject to change. Please contact the specific program of interest for the most current information on program details and costs.

Library of Congress Cataloging-in-Publication Data

Davis, Scott (Scott Mitchell).
    Living Jonathan's life : a doctor's descent into darkness and addiction /
Scott Davis.
    p. cm.
    ISBN-13: 978-0-7573-0649-5 (trade paper)
    ISBN-10: 0-7573-0649-7 (trade paper)
    1. Davis, Scott (Scott Mitchell), 1961—-Health. 2. Davis, Jonathan,
1961-1993—Health. 3. Physicians—United States—Drug use. 4. Physicians—
United States—Biography. 5. AIDS (Disease)—Patients—United States—
Biography. 6. Brothers—United States—Biography. I. Title.
    RC564.5.M45D38 2008
    362.196'97920092—dc22
    [B]

2007037729

Publisher: Health Communications, Inc.
         3201 S.W. 15th Street
         Deerfield Beach, FL 33442-8190

Cover photo © Image Source
Cover design by Larissa Hise Henoch
Interior design and formatting by Dawn Von Strolley Grove

Contents

Prologue

On July 23, 1993, my identical twin brother, Jonathan, lost his courageous battle with AIDS. Death was not new to me; I had lost other relatives and friends before and had felt a bit more alone in the world when each had passed. But the day I watched my twin brother die before my eyes, I experienced a loss that was devastating and without comparison. With his passing, I lost much more than a best friend, a confidante, and a brother; I lost a human mirror, a reflection into which I had always been able to look and from which I could gain strength. When Jonathan died, that once-radiant mirror turned black as stone. I could no longer see myself as I did before, let alone see myself living without him. His disease had claimed me, too.

In the early aftermath of his death, had I simply confronted the overwhelming grief that I was feeling, this book might never have been written. But I could not allow myself to grieve. At the time, I was a physician nearing completion of an internal medicine residency—the last of thirteen years of medical studies. I simply could not take a detour from completing them. The proverbial golden ring of academic success was finally in my grasp, and I was determined not to let go. Facing what seemed like bottomless grief over Jonathan's death was too monstrous at that point. I thought my anguished, thread-bare emotions would not be compatible in a career place where death and dying were commonplace. So I did the unthink-able—I swallowed my pain and grief and locked them inside.

I was different, I thought. Intelligent and strongwilled, I chose to swallow my pain as one would swallow pieces of steak too tough and difficult to chew. I would move on and digest Jonathan's death later, I reasoned. In doing so, however, I unknowingly ignited a bonfire inside myself.

I found ways to temporarily douse the searing flames of pain, though. Nightly sleeping pills removed any need to lie awake at night and replay Jonathan's death or ponder how I would live without him. One tablet gave me some relief from my burning grief. It was so easy.

The pills helped for a while, but the pain continued to smolder inside; there was no pill that could completely douse the grief-fueled fire in my gut. Chronic abdominal pain set in, baffling even the medical experts for a diagnosis. Numerous hospitalizations and procedures to alleviate the pain proved futile.

I received prescriptions for narcotics to ease my pain. These pills only deepened my desire to self-medicate and kept me from meditating on the real problem. Eventually, I found myself beginning to live a life similar to the kind Jonathan himself had suffered—one characterized by chronic pain, iso-lation, and an addiction to sedatives and narcotics. I, too, began to suffer the same physical and emotional pain he had tried to escape.

Our diseases had different names—it was AIDS for him and addiction for me—but our suffering was the same. Our outcomes would have been the same, too, if not for a sudden intervention, where I would be forced to finally confront the fiery demons of grief.

In an ironic twist of fate, I would come to draw strength and courage to rebuild my own life from a most unexpected source—Jonathan's secret poetry, kept hidden until after his death. The mysteries of who he really was and what I was to become would be revealed at a crossroads in my crisis.

I wanted to live. The more I came to understand my brother, the more I was able to honor his memory, his life, and to understand my own.

This book is the true story of identical twin brothers, each fighting similar physical and emotional battles. One would lose his life; the other would be nearly consumed by self-destructive grief.

I wanted to live.

Blessed is the man who finds wisdom,
the man who gains understanding,
for she is more profitable than silver
and yields better returns than gold.

—Proverbs 3:13–14 NIV

For Jonathan
His Poetry and His Valor
Will Live in Our Hearts Forever.

August 16, 1961–July 23, 1993

—*Jonathan's Epitaph*

Love Like the Universe

Love, like the universe, is magnificent.
Great not only in size
But perhaps even more in worth.
For true, the universe is contained of many mysteries,
Puzzling those who often seek to conquer it—challenge it.
Yet the simplicity and complexity of Love
Can be conquered by all—the strong, the poor, the rich, and the weak.

Love is as dark as the midnight sky
And as bright as the brilliancy of a noonday sun.
It lies not within the atmosphere to see or to touch
But is captured only within the Heaven of the Heart,
Sensing Love's unique emotion.

When Love calls, all that hear its magical tune listen,
Awaiting the sound of the pure bells
And the gentleness of the flute
That whispers to its followers.
But when the mournful beat of unforeseen drums
Crashes upon this beauty of songs,
Then the painful rhythm of this merciless beat
Threatens to crush all poetry
Love once thought to be strong.

But when Love again renews itself
It builds the greatest castles of the universe,
To protect its inner beauty
Against the beat of the defeated drums.

Love, like the universe, has but one common element
That guides the planets
As well as those in love.

The link is eternity
And eternity is universal.

—Jonathan Elliot Davis

1

The Mournful Beat of Unforeseen Drums

July 23, 1993

*T*he dream is always the same.

Jonathan and I are eight years old again, happy, laughing, running down a sidewalk in our quiet New Jersey neighborhood. The summer sun is bright and warm on our backs as we run to nowhere in particular. Just to be able to run seems good enough. I run behind Jonathan in tandem with his steps, as though the movement of my feet depends on his.

We race across a neighbor's lawn and cut into a narrow alleyway between two houses. We are still laughing childishly as the cold, dark recess seems to swallow us up, sweeping us toward the other side. As we near the end of the alleyway, the sunlight becomes even brighter and warmer than before. Somehow, I am now ahead of my brother as I rush into the light, arms raised and waving wildly, yelling, "Heeeere weee gooo! Heeeere weee gooo!"

I run into a large field I know well. It is dotted with small, grassy knolls and scattered with beautiful sunflowers. But I can no longer hear Jonathan running behind me. I turn around to urge him on faster.

Jonathan is running to catch up, but he is no longer an eight-year-old boy. He is thirty-three years old, as when I last saw him, and his body is frail with pain and illness. His eyes and face are sunken and discolored, pasty and ashen in tone. His clothes hang loosely around his wilted limbs. With a tired arm, Jonathan motions me to run ahead, and I dash behind one of the grassy hills. I lay flat behind the small hill, frightened by my brother's sudden transformation. Cautiously, I peer around it.

Jonathan is gone. I am alone in the field.

SHERMAN OAKS MEDICAL CENTER
Sherman Oaks, California

On July 23, 1993, I awoke once again from that dream. I had fallen asleep in the small dark hospital library. I was alone in the room, breathing in the musty smell of the worn leather couch where I had slept. A ray of obnoxiously bright fluorescent light intruded through the doorway and cut the serenity of the darkness. I feared that my life would change forever when I left this room, and I did not want to leave.

Knowing I could not stay, though, I walked out of that calm cocoon and into a torrent of frenzied activity. Nurses and doctors breezed by, seemingly oblivious to my presence as I made my way down the hallway to the intensive care unit.

From the crowded nurse's station, Jonathan's physician, Dr.

Gottlieb, looked up at me. He nodded and smiled weakly, but in his eyes was a sadness and sympathy that had not been there before. With his head, he motioned to me in the direction of Jonathan's room. I anxiously quickened my pace.

I was horrified by what I saw when I entered his room. In the dim early morning light of the intensive care unit, Jonathan lay in bed, eyes closed. A large plastic tube snaked out from a unit near his bed to a clear mask on his face. As the unit hissed in time with his shallow respirations, it forced concentrated oxygen into his weakened lungs. A heart monitor above his head showed his irregular heartbeat. Two steel intravenous poles on either side of him were so laden with clear and colored bags and bottles of medication that they resembled decorated Christmas trees. It was an ominous sign.

For a moment I just watched him, my heart heavy and quickly sinking. His skin, pinker and more vibrant just yesterday, was now a waxy, ashen yellow. It seemed to just drape over his face and arms. His eye sockets were dark and sunken. Jonathan opened his eyes and slowly scanned over to me.

He spoke in a voice that was barely audible. "Hi, Scott. You look pretty tired. Did you stay here all night?"

"Yeah, I slept in the library," I answered. "It just got too late to go home, that's all." I smiled at him, lying, knowing I never would have left. I'm sure he knew that.

"Always the diehard," he said, barely able to draw a smile.

I asked, "Did you sleep at all last night?"

"A little bit. The sleeping pill helped, but all this machine noise didn't."

"Yeah, I'll bet it didn't. You always did wake up at the drop of a pin."

Jonathan laughed for a moment. Then he began to cough violently for a few long seconds. His bedside blood oxygen monitor suddenly showed a precipitous drop in his oxygen levels: 90 . . . 89 . . . 88 . . . 87 . . . 86 . . . Less and less oxygen was being delivered to his blood. His lungs were barely doing their job.

I was about to run out and get the nurse when he stopped coughing. The monitor numbers began to inch back up as Jonathan took some deep breaths through the mask.

"Hate when that happens," he said with a faint smile.

I knew that must have frightened him, but I also knew he would be the last to show his fear to anyone, including me. Stonewall Jonathan!

I decided against my better judgment to leave the hospital for a while to shower and rest at my mother's house nearby. I needed to clear my head and briefly relax from the stress of the situation. Jonathan's condition seemed stable for now, I thought, and he would probably continue to improve as he had in past hospital visits. Despite what I had seen, I left actually feeling somewhat hopeful.

I arrived at my mother's house in Northridge twenty minutes later. She and my stepfather, Bob, had remained at the hospital, so the house was quiet. As I walked upstairs to the bathroom, the phone rang. I ran into the master bedroom to answer it, fearing the call.

Pat, a close friend of our family, was calling from the hospital. Her voice was unsteady. "You have to come back right now! Jonathan's taken a turn for the worse!" My frantic drive to the hospital was a horrible mix of blazing speed, anxiety, and an impending fear that this would become the worst day of my life. That sense of doom grew stronger as I weaved in and out of street traffic and rocketed into the hospital parking lot.

Shortly I was back in Jonathan's room. My mother and Bob, my stepfather; my father and his wife, Diane; and two close family friends, Pat and Sandie, all stood in a circle around my brother's bed. I went to Jonathan's side. His eyes were closed. His breathing was rapid and irregular. Each breath was labored. His nurse came in somberly and silently injected more Valium into his IV and turned up his morphine pump to sedate him. I knew at that moment my twin brother was dying.

But when the mournful beat of unforeseen drums
Crashes upon this beauty of songs,
Then the painful rhythm of this merciless beat
Threatens to crush all poetry
Love once thought to be strong.

Jonathan's body began to relax and his breathing quieted. The pained, furrowed expression on his face began to smooth out and take on a more peaceful countenance. I held his hand, whispering, "It's okay, Jon, we're all here. Just go to sleep now," still feeling the strength of one of his fingers pressing my palm. I believe he was acknowledging that he understood. Then Jonathan took a short, gasping breath. It was his last.

I don't remember how long I cried from that moment on, but it seemed like an hour. At that moment, I not only felt the heart-wrenching pain of losing my twin brother, but of losing a part of myself too. Part of my identity since childhood was "us" as identical twins, one flesh and blood, one unique bond. At that moment, I never felt as close to my own fragile mortality as I did to his.

Jonathan and I were both in the comforting company of our loved ones. But I was alone in the field again.

Memory of Autumn

Remember the days of moments past
That fade from memory like withered grass,
The simple pleasures—once a smile, now a sigh,
Those childhood questions that found no reply,
The corner drugstore in the late afternoon,
That old Victrola playing somber, faded tunes.

Remember the sunrise, now see how it sets,
That sun shined brightly to dim all regrets,
Those birds that once sang to children each day,
That laughter—that sun—it was destined to stay,
The young never cried and the old never sinned.
But the memory of autumn is caught by the wind.

Ah, how one remembers the days that fell like rain,
The morn' that brought the sunshine—
the eve that witnessed pain.
Ages that time has lost from sight, some hold with their mind.
Yet though life seems to keep most well, many hearts are blind.
For love is blocked by virgin hearts, and value marred by time.

Rising from our tired swings, we move across the porch,
The dark sky holds our anguish—we no longer bear the torch,
Indeed we laugh for all the days a tear could not detain.
And one who laughs resolves the truth
Then sadly weeps again.
For the memory of autumn is caught quickly by the wind.

Remember the days of moments past.
They bloom like roses
Then break like glass.

—Jonathan Elliot Davis

2

Days of Moments Past

*J*onathan, where are you going?" my mother called. Then louder, she called, "I said, where are you going?"

"Nowhere, Mommy!" Jonathan cried back as we ran into the front yard and down to the sidewalk. "Just out to play for a while!"

"Well, be careful!" we heard her say. "And don't you two go near the creek. It's dangerous there."

Jonathan and I said in unison, as we so often did, "Okay, Mommy, we won't!" As we ran, we smiled at each other, also thinking in unison, "Yeah, the creek! Let's go!"

My brother and I had been born eight years earlier in a Flushing, New York, hospital to our parents, Joel and Sheila, who already had a two-year-old, Neil. In utero, Jonathan and I lay so close together and our heartbeats were so synchronized that only one heartbeat could be heard during pregnancy.

Needless to say, our parents had been expecting only one baby. In the hospital waiting room, on hearing a nurse's news that "the twins are doing fine," my grandmother Sally asked incredulously, "What do you mean, 'twins'?" Then she fainted.

From that day on, Jonathan and I were known as "The Twins" to our friends and relatives.

When our mother had her way, she dressed us alike, but I was always "the heavier one" to anyone who attempted to make a distinction between us. But no matter how we were dressed or how people referred to us, Jonathan and I knew that our likeness was truly our uniqueness in the world. We were separate children, of course, but so close that we knew what the other one was thinking or could say one word and burst out laughing. We were "The Twins" and that was all that mattered.

The infamous creek we were headed to that afternoon in New Jersey was only about a quarter mile from our house—easily within the range of two adventurous eight-year-old boys. As our mother knew, the creek was indeed dangerous; it had a very tall concrete culvert that spanned over it, creating an immense and dark channel that the creek drained into. The edge of the culvert sloped downward and could easily send a young child tumbling twenty feet into the creek below. Mom had warned Jonathan and me of the danger many times, but, of course, that only made it seem more mysterious and appealing.

When we got to the culvert, we stopped and stood on its flat ledge, overlooking the steep slope. We watched the creek below. Its waters narrowed and merged into frothy little whitecaps before vanishing into the gaping channel opening. It was scary and exciting at the same time.

On the far edge of the slope, someone had nailed a narrow, foot-long wooden board. The board hung over the edge precariously, like a teeter-totter. Jonathan took a few steps gingerly down the slope toward the board.

"Jon, don't go down there. You'll fall," I said nervously.

"Yeah, right!" he shot back. "I've been down here plenty times before. And don't tell Mom. She'd kill me and you just for being here." He reached the wooden board and stepped on it with one foot, teetering it back and forth.

"Jon, you're scaring me. Get back here!" I called.

"See, Scott? It can hold me up." He stepped on the board, lifted his other foot, and balanced himself, arms outstretched. "See, I can even—"

The board shifted forward and Jonathan fell over the edge, screaming as he plummeted twenty feet to the creek below. Then I heard nothing.

Frantically I slid to the edge and peered down. Incredibly, Jonathan was still sitting up, crying and staring into the huge, black mouth of the channel opening in front of him. I had never seen such terror on his face before. We were separated by something monstrous for the first time in our young lives. I didn't know it then, but it would not be the last time.

I ran off the culvert and tore back to our street, screaming, "My brother fell in the creek! My brother fell in the creek!" Tears sailed off my cheeks as I raced toward home. Drawn by the magnet of my cries, several neighbors dashed into the street and toward the culvert. A couple of the men had probably been interrupted from watching TV or working in their yards and had dashed outside shirtless. My mother heard the commotion before I even reached my door, and I turned around and ran back toward the creek with her and the small rescue party.

Minutes later, the neighbors had lifted Jonathan to the top of the culvert. Miraculously, he suffered only a few minor abrasions on his legs and buttocks, and our mother's angry tongue-lashing as she dragged us home in her tight grip. I hadn't fallen in the creek as he had, but I had tasted his terror, for we thought and felt alike.

3

Bloom Like Roses,
Break Like Glass

"The drive to my mother's house from the funeral was around fifteen minutes long, but it seemed like forever. I actually smiled a little when we pulled into the driveway in the limo."

"You smiled?" Dr. Miota asked. A grin of her own lit her face. Psychiatrists always love to have something to dig into. Maybe she thought she had found something to explore.

"Yeah, I did. I was thinking about my mother leading Jon away from that culvert. I felt sorry for him, but I was also glad it wasn't me who was in so much trouble. We really had a good childhood, and sometimes those little flashbacks make it . . . easier."

"Easier to deal with the pain of losing him?"

I sat there on the couch, silent. On hearing the words "losing him," another wave of clenching, overwhelming grief began to grip me and my eyes welled up. My mind raced to find another happier childhood moment that could somehow fill the dark void and ease what I was feeling. I didn't want to start crying again. I just wanted to be happy, even if just for a moment.

"Scott, it's not good to hold back. You need to let go of what you're feeling."

Damn psychiatrists! I thought.

Still knee-deep in my silence, Dr. Miota continued, "So, what happened after the funeral, at your mother's home? Lots of people there, I'd imagine."

"Yeah, there were quite a few. But it was hard for me to be around them at the time. I really just wanted to be alone. So I went upstairs to Jon's room and looked around. You know, it was the last place he'd been with me before he left for the hospital."

"Kind of like going back to a safer place? Before everything suddenly changed for you?"

"Exactly. But it was still hard. Everything in the room was as he'd left it—IV bottles with his AIDS medications and anti-biotics, drawers full of syringes, needles, bagged fluids—like a pharmacy. He really suffered at the end, I think . . . " My voice grew raspy and trailed off. *Think of something happy. Don't get pulled down again.*

Dr. Miota continued with her version of the Inquisition. "It must have been especially hard being a twin to have seen him in that condition. Did he ever talk to you about how he was feeling?"

No, never! He didn't, and at that moment, I couldn't bring myself to talk about my own feelings either. The doctor was trying to lead me down a path I just couldn't take.

There was a long, calculated pause until the doctor tried another path. "So, tell me about you and Jonathan in Boston," she said. "You said that was when you first found out he was HIV-positive. You must have had some good times together then, too." I was still searching my mind for happier times, but Dr. Miota knew just how to reach for both the happiness and the grief.

I suddenly remembered being with Jon in Boston. We were together once again, and the night air had never seemed so cold, yet so inviting.

Remember the days of moments past.
They bloom like roses
Then break like glass.

BOSTON, MASSACHUSETTS
July 1, 1990

The sushi at Takashima restaurant was the best in Boston, and Jon and I knew our sushi. It was a bit of a costly meal for me at that time, as I was then a third-year medical student on a fixed income. But sushi was something Jonathan and I really enjoyed sharing. That alone made it worth the price.

We were sitting together at the small, crowded sushi bar, a half dozen empty little plates in front of each of us. The sushi had been delicious, and the soothing bottle of warm sake I had enjoyed with my dinner was just starting to numb my brain and fingers. My belly was full, I was in my brother's company, and I was only one year away from medical school graduation. Life was good.

"So what do you say we blow this pop stand?" Jon asked. "If I sit here five more minutes, I'm gonna be starving again for more sushi. And at these prices, you'll have to take out another student loan," he smiled. "Anyway, I have to be up early tomorrow for work." Jon had recently found a job as a radiation safety officer at Boston University where I was attending school.

"Okay, then. Let's hit the road," I said. We rose from our seats and the sushi chefs began their high-pitched chorus of good-byes in Japanese.

Ten minutes later, I pulled up in front of Jonathan's apartment in Allston. We sat in silence in the car for a few moments. A light summer rain began to pelt the windshield.

Jon broke the silence. "You remember I'm going back to California tomorrow to visit Mom and Dad for a few days, right?"

"Yeah, I'll take care of your apartment and the cat," I said, saving him the effort of asking for the favor. That was one of the many nice things about being Jonathan's twin—our mental telepathy saved us a lot of unnecessary talk. Each of us just knew what the other was thinking!

"Thanks," he said. "Here's the key. I leave tomorrow morning, so come by tomorrow night to make sure Allston hasn't trashed the place. And don't forget her bedtime treats." Jon adored his cat, Allston. Jonathan was a bit of a loner and had no friends that I knew about, but that cat was his cherished companion.

"Will do," I said as he got out of the car. "I'll call you in California. By the way, does Allston prefer sushi or sashimi with her kitty chow?" We laughed and Jonathan pushed the door shut. I drove off watching Jon in the rearview mirror. He was getting wet in the rain, but he stood there just the same, watching me drive away.

My life would never be the same after that night.

> *Remember the sunrise, now see how it sets,*
> *That sun shined brightly to dim all regrets,*
> *Those birds that once sang to children each day,*
> *That laughter—that sun—it was destined to stay,*
> *The young never cried and the old never sinned.*
> *But the memory of autumn is caught by the wind . . .*

The next morning was like any other for me, except my outlook was different. I was doing my usual morning drive from my apartment to Boston University Medical Center. After two years of trekking back and forth, my car could have almost driven itself there, but that day was different; it was the start of my last year of medical school. I *was* a senior medical student!

In the grand scheme of things, of course, I was still on the bottom of the medical totem pole and I knew it. But little by little, I was rising higher, and it felt good. It seemed nothing that day could have changed my good mood.

I stopped at a stoplight and happened to glance down at the passenger seat next to me. A tiny pill was wedged into the bottom seat fold. I picked it up and looked at it for a moment. I recognized its distinctive shape. It was AZT, the pill then most commonly used to treat HIV disease.

I started to rack my brain, trying to remember who I'd had in the car with me recently. I had driven my classmate Ted home two days ago. *It must be his!* I thought. I wanted to know for sure, but I thought it might be rude of me and embarrassing for him if I asked him outright. I tucked the pill in my pocket and tried to forget about it, but I couldn't think of much else the rest of my drive.

Later that morning, I bumped into Ted after I had finished my morning rounds with the radiology chief. For better or worse, I had to ask him.

"Ted, this may seem strange," I stammered, "but I found something in my car this morning and was wondering if it was yours." Ted looked puzzled and then even more so as I produced the single pill from my pocket.

He stared for a minute, and then asked, "What is that?"

"It's AZT."

Ted just stared at me in disbelief for a moment, his eyes narrowing angrily. Finally, he spat, "What do you think, I'm some kind of fag?" Then more quietly he muttered, "Go to hell, Davis," and marched off.

I stood there in the corridor feeling both guilty and confused. I had insulted Ted and would have to try to patch things up with him. Worse yet, the pill belonged to someone, but who?

———————

"So what happened that night that changed your life?" Dr. Miota asked, jarring my stream of thoughts.

I hesitated, not really wanting to go there, not wanting to relive the painful past. *Isn't this session with her almost over already?* I thought. But the truth was, I had already begun to relive the past, and somehow I trusted her with my memories. I continued.

I found Ted later that day and apologized to him, but I had hurt his feelings badly. He accepted my apology, but I knew our friendship had taken a blow. I hoped things would smooth over in time. I liked Ted, and we had a lot in common—including our tendency to bruise easily.

I drove back to Jon's place that night, fighting the gnawing possibility that perhaps the AZT pill was his. I couldn't fathom it, but I had no other passengers in my car besides Ted. My thoughts swung back and forth. *Jon couldn't be sick! He doesn't show any of the signs.* I had just recently completed a rotation through the hospital's AIDS clinic (ironically, with Ted). I mentally recalled the signs of HIV infection—unexplained fever, night sweats, weight loss, anemia, history of blood transfusions, IV drug use, homosexual contact.

Then I began to recall things that tightened my gut even more. Jon had had a blood transfusion in a hospital several years back, after an extensive procedure to repair a broken nose. And once after that, he had passed out. The doctors had said it was due to anemia. *But he's my identical twin brother!* I told myself. *It can't be possible. It just can't be!*

By the time I reached Jon's apartment, I was practically on fire to find out the truth. I needed to find some piece of evidence that would deny or confirm my fears. I entered his apartment and Allston ran up to greet me. I think she was a bit miffed I didn't pet her and talk to her, but my mind was elsewhere. At least she hadn't wrecked the place. Jonathan would be happy about that.

I headed straight for Jonathan's bedroom. I knew from my medical training that an HIV-positive person will almost always receive a letter confirming their positive blood test result. I knew Jon kept almost everything and I also knew where.

I opened his desk drawer and pulled out the small file box he always kept pushed toward the back. I opened the lid. The envelope on top was addressed from a medical doctor's office in Boston. My fear soared as I pulled out the enclosed letter and read it, my hands trembling.

> *Dear Jonathan:*
>
> *With this letter, I regret to inform you that your blood test result was positive for antibodies to the human immunodeficiency virus (HIV), indicating that you have been infected with this virus. I urge you to schedule an appointment as soon as possible to begin treatment and follow-up. Please contact me at any time during office hours to discuss this.*
>
> *Sincerely,*
> *Dr. Robert Blane, M.D.*

I dropped the letter. It fluttered to the floor, taking my heart with it. My knees collapsed, and I sat on the floor and cried. My grief was only deepened by the fact that, as a medical student, I knew there was no real "treatment" for HIV. In the end, this virus had yet to spare almost anyone infected with it. AZT only temporarily stalled this progressive, terminal illness.

Wave after wave of grief swept over me. I knew what lay ahead for Jonathan—always one more treatment, one more blood test, one more illness after another, each worse than the one before. I cried and wondered why it had to happen to him—my twin brother. As always, I wept for us both.

They . . . break like glass . . .

I left Dr. Miota's office at the UCLA Neuropsychiatric Institute, still somewhat shaken after our conversation. It hurt to dig into that deep well of memories and relive the past—especially a past that I knew was filled with more and more pain and anguish. No, it was much easier just not to go there.

I arrived home at 11:00 PM. My wife, Rebecca, was sleeping, or pretending to. I went into the walk-in closet in our bedroom and found my hidden stash of sleeping pills. The memories still thrashing around in my brain would soon be chemically put to sleep, for a while anyway. I took a pill and went to bed.

Twenty minutes later, the pill began to take effect. Those haunting memories, stirred up like hot coals in Dr. Miota's hands, were cooling off. A warm cocoon of induced sleep enveloped me. Again.

An Echo Unheard

How often I've yearned to stand by the shore
On the rocks untouched by time and sea,
To hear a world speak with a violent roar,
Thus claiming it victor to every degree.

The sun burns high in its fiery blaze.
The wind whips the sea to whitened caps.
So small seem I to Nature's ways,
To live and die—a mortal's trap.

Forever shall these waters pound at the Earth
And lifetimes praise the beauty of waves.
Yet struggle must I from the moment of birth
To lift up my voice in these precious days.

I like the mountains that rise to such heights,
Then crumple like sand to the wind-beaten dust
By a force which towers any deity of might.
Through will I survive, then fall I must.
Eternity, true, succeeds the greatest of men.
As the days find their youth when I tremble with age.
Though I will perish—and Nature knows when
My Spirit shall hush the most powerful waves.

How great do I err in an ignorant course?
What regret do I know when, unspoken, I've wronged?
For to think of this Nature an incomparable force
When the blood of its Sea is the flesh of my Song!

—Jonathan Elliot Davis

4

The Flesh of My Song

*J*onathan loved the sea. He loved it so much, in fact, that he chose to make a career out of sailing on it. His love for the ocean physically separated us for years. But, ironically, his pursuit of the waves finally brought him back on land—and to Boston where I studied medicine.

As a young boy, Jon was fascinated by the sea. At age fourteen, he was encouraged by a family friend—a lieutenant commander in the navy—to join the Sea Cadets, the youth branch of that service. Jon jumped at the chance.

For the next several years, he relished the Sea Cadet outings on the ocean with passion, becoming a model member of the cadet force. With his exemplary service, at age seventeen, Jon was one of only two cadets selected for an around-the-world cruise on a navy Antarctic icebreaker, traveling to the bottom of the world and to far-off tropical ports some can only dream about. "The beauty and the raw power of the ocean courses through my veins now," Jon wrote in his journal of that trip. He was hooked for life.

This experience led him to pursue a career in the navy. He set his bearings on the Naval Academy in Annapolis, Maryland. He obtained a required, and glowing, recommendation for Academy admission by a U.S. congressman. But his prior high school academic performance did not meet the Academy's stringent admission criteria, and his application was rejected.

Jonathan was not about to let his less-than-stellar grades keep him from his beloved ocean. He applied to the Merchant Marine Academy in Vallejo, California. He was accepted, and he dove immediately into its rigorous curriculum—calculus, heat and fluid physics, marine engineering—subjects that would have stopped me well short of the school's entrance.

Jon was never a scholar himself by any stretch of the imagination. But he was a fighter, and he knew what he wanted. Unfortunately, he wanted much more than his academic ability would allow him. He failed several subjects over the course of two semesters and was dismissed from the program. Still, he refused to give up. One year later, after heavily petitioning the Academy to be reinstated, the officials decided to give him a second chance. Jon was matriculated back into the Merchant Marine Academy. A semester later, however, he had again failed several courses. This time, he was dismissed permanently.

Despite this setback, my brother's passion could not be daunted, so he enlisted in the U.S. Navy. Six weeks of winter boot camp training in Great Lakes, Illinois, did not deter him. He endured long military marches in subzero temperatures, crowded barracks, and five-minute meals. Jon endured a completely regimented existence, all in pursuit of his dream.

When he graduated from boot camp, Jonathan was accepted into the navy's prestigious nuclear engineering program in Mystic, Connecticut. It seemed that Jonathan would finally have a chance at his dream after all—to work in the ocean—navigating a naval nuclear submarine.

Though I was Jon's identical twin, I didn't share his love of the ocean. While he lived to ride the ocean waves, the mere thought sent my equilibrium into a deep-dive maneuver. While I was studying to be a doctor, Jon couldn't tolerate the sight of blood. We shared a love of science, but each of us was content to pursue it in completely different arenas.

Jonathan and I weren't always "A" students, but our determination made up for less-than-perfect grades. My performance as an undergraduate at the University of California, Davis, was satisfactory in the premedical courses that mattered for medical school admissions. But medical schools around the country wanted candidates with grades that were not just satisfactory, but stellar.

In 1984, after graduating from college, I tried to gain entrance to a U.S. medical school—by way of Mexico. The Autonomous University of Guadalajara in Mexico was a haven for American students who wanted to go to a U.S. medical school but couldn't gain entrance—a kind of home for wayward doctors-to-be! However, after a year of poorly taught first-year medical school courses and endless indigestion from the local food, I had had enough.

In July 1985, 1 was offered a spot in the master's program in physiology at Boston University. I would study alongside its medical students, complete my master's degree, and hopefully, if all went well, be accepted into Boston University Medical School's second-year class. That was my dream and my vision.

Jonathan's dream of naval nuclear engineering and my dream to go to a U.S. medical school were finally realized at nearly the same time! Things happened that way—we were twins, remember?

In 1988, six months after my graduation from the master's program, I proudly stepped into the lobby of Boston University Medical School. I was in!

Both Jonathan's and my pursuit of our dream careers had been long and circuitous. He and I, the inseparable "Twins," had taken separate career paths in different directions, but by some glorious twist of fate, we were finally pursuing them together. He had become a budding nuclear engineer in Connecticut, and I had become a medical student, just an hour's drive away in Boston. It seemed life had dealt each of us a pair of aces, and we were playing the same hand!

Two years later, I graduated from medical school. Jon, looking fit, robust, and proud, was there at my side with the rest of our family to celebrate my accomplishments. Our victories were each other's and we celebrated them together.

It was a bittersweet time for me, though, because by this time I had known about Jonathan's illness for an entire year. He still didn't know that I knew, and I still had not come to terms with it.

We were identical twin brothers. The blood of his sea was the flesh of my song, and I never wanted that music to stop.

As Far as the Sun

If love could be measured as far as the sun,
And daydreams be valued as priceless as gold,
Then my journey to your heart I know I have done.
For the weight of your karats is too great to have sold.

Wishes like water run free down a stream,
Hope can surge miles from the seas to the stars.
This love that we've captured in a looking-glass dream
Is that wish-I-may star shine we now claim to be ours.

There are riches in friendship.
There is power in love
Beyond fortunes in wealth we have won.
Still, if answers seem hopeless in what we search for,
Know our love can be measured just as far as the sun.

—Jonathan Elliot Davis

5

A Looking-Glass Dream

No one was to know about Jonathan's illness. No one. That was the edict my mother gave me when I told her about the letter I found in his apartment.

"It will be Jonathan's decision when he decides to tell the family," she said. "And don't tell him that you know, either. He just doesn't want *anyone* to know!"

I was hurt, but I could understand Jon not wanting me to know. An amazing thing about being his twin was that it was easy for me to put myself in his shoes—to think what he thought, to feel what he felt. So better than anyone, I understood why he did what he did. He didn't want me to know about his illness for fear that my feelings for him would somehow change. I truly was his flesh and blood—the one thing that, above all, he didn't want to change. Jonathan's whole world had suddenly changed, and he didn't want me to be part of that upheaval. So he kept me out. But I also knew that *I, too, was keeping him out*, and I fought my burning desire to talk to him. I remained silent, even though I *desperately* wanted to open up to him.

I wanted to reach out to him, to be able to tell him I would be there for him, even if he thought no one else would be. I wanted him to know that our relationship, our brotherly love, would never change in spite of his illness. I wanted us to eat our sushi dinners, see good movies the instant they opened, take vacations—together—like we used to. I knew Jon's disease was like a pointed pendulum hanging over him, waiting to drop. But he was in good health for now, so I thought. I wanted us to enjoy it.

UNIVERSITY OF CALIFORNIA, IRVINE MEDICAL CENTER
October 1991

I thought that once I graduated from medical school in May 1991, my internship in internal medicine would be the lesser of my dues to pay before I went into private practice. It wasn't. The final two years of my medical school training were tantamount to paying an exorbitant amount of money to work long hours with no paycheck. My internship was even worse—I earned a miniscule amount of money for working twice as many hours with double the responsibility. I had jumped from the proverbial frying pan into the fire, and I felt like I was coated with flammable liquid, too.

October tenth of that year started out as a routine day; I

attended the morning patient rounds as I always did with Dr. Auslander, the chief of service, and two other interns. We three interns had been assigned to the patients on the hematologyoncology service that month, and so far, it had not been as grueling as many of our other internship rotations—there were no overnight hospital calls, there was a relatively light patient load, and the oncology resident working with us was a perfectionist who did most of the work. It was an easy assignment that we stressed-out interns happily accepted. We needed a break.

The rotation wasn't entirely a piece of cake, though. Dr. Auslander was known for verbally cutting into any intern who wasn't prepared. So we had already gotten into the habit of coming two hours early to help one another review and prepare.

Dr. Auslander marched into the first patient's room that morning like he always did—at precisely 8:00 AM. You could practically set your watch by his arrival time. His long white, heavily starched coat matched his crisp, almost militant gait as he strutted in. I stood at attention with my fellow interns, clipboard in hand, patient information fresh in my mind. I was ready for whatever questions he might throw at me.

Dr. Auslander strode up to the bedside like a general about to be debriefed. "Begin, Dr. Davis," he said to me. "Oh, hello, Mrs. McCarthy," he said to the patient before nodding at me to begin. He closed his eyes while listening to me, as though to assimilate every single word.

I began to tell him about the patient. Mrs. McCarthy had metastatic breast cancer. Her chemotherapy had briefly slowed the progression of her cancer. However, after four rounds of the treatment, her own immune system had become so weakened that the chemotherapy had been stopped. Like a lion unleashed after being restrained for a while, the cancer had then attacked with a vengeance, metastasizing quickly to her lungs and bone. The morphine dripping from a pump into her intravenous line was a clear sign of the extent of her disease. She also closed her eyes while I talked; she, like Dr. Auslander, was listening intently, but every word was life itself for Mrs. McCarthy.

I completed my bedside review, mentioning Mrs. McCarthy's level of pain, physical examination, and lab work for the morning. Dr. Auslander then motioned to me to continue our talk outside her room.

"Increase her morphine drip, Dr. Davis," he said. "As you mentioned, her CAT scan shows that the brain metastasis is enlarging. She *is* deteriorating. Her family needs to know." With that, he spun around and turned into the next patient's room before I had a chance to nod in agreement. His approach to a dying patient had to be *our* approach—professional and completely detached.

Unfortunately, there were many Mrs. McCarthys on this service and under my care—all sick like my brother, all with families who cared for them as I did for him. In their eyes I saw Jonathan. Would he meet the same desperate fate? Would he let me be there for him?

Seeing Mrs. McCarthy that day caused something to click inside me. Her family needed to know about her, and after eighteen months of silence about Jonathan's illness, I needed Jonathan to know that I was there. That day, I decided to tell him I knew. But as it turned out, I wouldn't have to.

The next day, I had just completed my morning rounds with

Dr. Auslander when my pager beeped. It was the hospital operator.

"Dr. Davis, I have an urgent call for you," she said as I called from a small anteroom near the nurse's station. "Your mother is calling from Chicago."

Chicago? Jon had moved there only several months before to begin a new job with a company managing nuclear and toxic waste. Why would she be calling from there? The operator connected me at once.

"Scott, it's Mom. Listen, I'm with Jonathan at Northwestern University Hospital in Chicago. Here, he wants to talk to you." There was a long pause as she passed the phone to him.

"Hi, Scott," Jon finally said. His voice sounded very tired and weak. He coughed loudly for a few seconds, then added, "I have to tell you something. You know that I'm HIV-positive, don't you?"

He knew that I knew! Why had I waited so long to bring it up? "Yes, Jon, I know," I said softly. I felt guilty for not speaking to him much sooner. But he was calling from the hospital, and I feared there would be much more to this conversation.

Jon then revealed, "I was admitted with pneumonia. They did some tests and found it was PCP." He paused, waiting for the words to sink in. *Pneumocystis carinii pneumonia.* There were a few drawbacks to being a doctor; sometimes I knew more than I wanted to. I knew full well what PCP meant; Jonathan now had a full-blown AIDS infection. His words sunk deep to the bottom of my heart and pulled it down hard.

I thought to myself, *Oh, God, is this the beginning of the end?* But I said to him, "Don't worry, I'm sure your doctors will knock that out of you and send you home, right?"

"Oh, yeah," he replied, "and they said it wasn't too bad. A couple of days and I'll be out."

"Good," I said. "Just enough time for Allston to really trash your furniture."

Jon laughed. It was good to hear him laugh, but I knew he must have been very scared. Most people who developed full-blown AIDS died within a few years after they were diagnosed. Knowing Jonathan, I was sure he had already done the research and knew the dismal facts. But new treatments for AIDS were on the horizon, and Jonathan had Dr. Michael Gottlieb, one of the best doctors in the country for AIDS patients. There *was* hope, I told myself.

After a few minutes of chatting, Jon sounded better and I felt better. I said good-bye and promised to visit him in Chicago soon. As I hung up the phone, Jon's hopeful voice disconnected and I found myself staring down a hall filled with terminal cancer patients. Reality set in again.

There are riches in friendship.
There is power in love
Beyond fortunes in wealth we have won.
Still, if answers seem hopeless in what we search for,
Know our love can be measured just as far as the sun.

My thoughts were interrupted by a nurse's voice calling my name.

"Dr. Davis?" she implored, briskly and breathlessly walking up to me. "Mrs. McCarthy is having more pain, and her breathing is becoming labored."

6

As Far as the Sun

*T*here are distinct advantages to being an identical twin, especially when you are growing up. When you look almost exactly like your sibling, you can make good use of that when the moment calls for it. For example, let's say you don't want to go to a certain class one day. You simply trade classes with your twin and enjoy a day off. Or if you need a break from talking with your long-winded girlfriend on the phone, you can let your twin talk to her instead. The two of you think alike anyway, so he'll know what to say. And if you ever get in trouble with your parents, there's always the chance they will punish your twin for it. Having Jonathan as my identical twin, of course, meant more to me than just being able to switch identities with him when it suited me; he was truly a unique gift from God. Jonathan had his own thoughts, his own dreams, and his own talents. But I always felt blessed at being able to share my young life with someone so much like myself. It is said that we humans spend our lives searching for others similar to ourselves. I had been given a soul mate at birth.

Many cultures have rites of passage for young people— milestones that mark the next phase of life. For Jewish boys, the bar mitzvah service is one of the most important. In the span of a two-hour religious ceremony, a Jewish boy who is turning thirteen becomes a man, at least in principle. It is an often nerve-racking rite of passage that a Jewish boy must face by himself—unless he has an identical twin.

Jonathan and I were born and raised Jewish.

As the date of our bar mitzvah service approached, Jonathan and I were happy to be able to divide the many bar mitzvah prayers, readings, and incantations between us. We were to read these aloud in front of several hundred temple congregants at our bar mitzvah ceremony. Once again, I thought, I would enjoy a benefit of being a twin!

On bar mitzvah day, the ceremony went smoothly—that is, until it was Jonathan's turn to speak. The rabbi rose from his chair on the temple stage and walked over to Jonathan. My brother stood at the pulpit, crouched over an open Torah scroll, ready to recite from it as he had prepared for months to do. "Jonathan will now read from our Holy Scriptures," the rabbi announced proudly, and nodded for him to begin.

Instead, Jonathan simply stood there, frozen. Staring out at a well-dressed sea of family, relatives, friends, and spectators, he became paralyzed with fear and could not remember nor utter a single word. I squirmed in my seat with embarrassment, fearing Jonathan would ruin the whole thing for the both of us and we would have to do it all over again. I guess it was a little sacrilegious, but as I sat there in the temple, I prayed I would not have to spend one more day in Hebrew school to prepare for another bar mitzvah!

Finally, the rabbi gently and sympathetically pushed Jonathan aside to read the prayers for him, and the service continued. In the end, we were both bar mitzvahed, we did not have to suffer the pain of more Hebrew school, and most importantly, we got to keep all of our bar mitzvah gifts. For two thirteen-year-old boys, the latter was most important at the time.

———✦———

Dr. Miota jostled me back to reality. She knew just how to bridge the gap that I was in, between my happier childhood moments and my grief over the recent past. It was so much easier being on the happier side.

"You like going back there, don't you?" she said.

"Back where?"

"Back to your memories, the good ones—the ones that keep you from dealing with your feelings today." *There she goes again. Let out some psychobabble fishing line and then reel me back in for another harpooning.* But Dr. Miota was right. She always was.

I sat on her comfortable leather couch in silence for a few moments and hoped the good doctor would turn the conversation toward something more pleasant. My agony over Jonathan's death still loomed within me like a bottomless pit. I preferred to go anywhere but so close to its slippery edges, where I might fall in and have to actually deal with my feelings!

Dr. Miota changed the topic, but toward one even less pleasant.

"Scott, when *did* you finally stop taking the sleeping pills?"

"About two weeks ago, when I started coming here," I lied. I had taken one the previous night, as I would that night. I hated myself for lying to her. *But I needed the damn things!*

"Very good," she said, "and you're sleeping well at night?"

"Very well!" I said, which was the truth.

———◦•◦———

Jonathan was still relatively healthy. He recovered quickly from that first bout of PCP and went back to work. However, with my knowledge that he finally had a full AIDS infection, *I* could not recover as quickly. My performance as an intern on the hematologyoncology service began to suffer. My once sharp, concise morning reports to Dr. Auslander became more and more disjointed, sometimes even confusing. I was on the verge of failing this internship rotation. Even if I passed, I knew my evaluation from Dr. Auslander would not be a kind one. I decided to tell Dr. Auslander what was going on.

"Take a week off to visit your brother in Chicago," he told me as I sat with him in his office. It was December 1991, three weeks before the rotation ended. "I'll pass you for this rotation, but not with flying colors, you understand?" I nodded and smiled thankfully. I had been granted an academic stay of execution.

Failing an internship rotation would have set my residency back several months. Dr. Auslander—my by-the-book, militant commander—was being very generous with me, and I would take what I could get. I left his office feeling like I had won a battle, but the war was just beginning.

7

The Tamer of the Lion

*T*he first time I went out to visit Jonathan in Chicago that December 1991, the winter air was brutal. When I stepped off the plane and into the terminal at O'Hare International Airport, the floor-to-ceiling windows were thick with frost and condensation. As I walked down the corridor to meet Jon at the other end, it seemed as though the windows were growing more opaque and less transparent by the minute. It was an eerie feeling, as though the corridor was closing in around me.

Then I saw Jonathan standing at the end of the walkway waiting for me. He looked great. He seemed a little thinner than usual, but healthy, as though he had never been sick a day in his life. His short dark-blond hair, like mine, was starting to gray at the sides. His complexion was clear and his face rosy and cherubic. I knew all of that would change as his illness progressed, but for now I was thrilled that he looked so well.

For the first time in as long as I could remember, Jonathan and I hugged each other. Still holding on to me, he looked at me with his trademark half-crooked smile—the left corner of his lips pulled up, the right corner pulled down as if to say, "It's great to see you, Scott, but what's this really all about?"

I was scared out of my wits that he had AIDS. I wondered where it would lead him and how fast it would take him there. But whatever happened, I would be there for him. I didn't have to tell him that; he was my twin and he already knew it. Wordlessly, we picked up my luggage at the baggage claim and ventured into the frozen-over tundra called Chicago.

The weather that week was especially brutal, but Jon's warmth as a brother and host made it much more bearable. Jonathan took me on a whirlwind tour of the city. We saw Chicago's famous Museum of Science, with its replica mineshaft that plunged us six floors underground; we drove along Lakeside Drive at Lake Michigan; we passed by the Biograph Theater, where the gangster John Dillinger was gunned down by the FBI; and we ate real Chicago-style pizza. With each new adventure in his city, Jonathan bubbled with pride at introducing me to his turf. Happily, I soaked up every minute with him, just content that he was healthy enough to enjoy it.

It was just Jonathan and me all week, laughing, joking, teasing, and reminiscing. At one point, we ran along the icy sidewalk on crowded Michigan Avenue just as we had done as kids. It felt as though "The Twins" were back together, better than ever, and there was no stopping us! My mind even played with a precious glimmer of hope that Jon could beat his dreaded disease.

Our laughter calmed down and the conversation took a more serious turn as we sat in a restaurant eating our second pizza dinner of the week.

"So, Jon, how do you think this happened?" I asked him cautiously after a long pause in the conversation.

"What?" he replied, knowing very well what I was asking.

"How do you think you got the virus?"

Jonathan stared at his plate for a while before answering. "I think it must have been from that blood transfusion, the one I got after I broke my nose. Bad blood or something." He shifted uncomfortably in his seat. We rarely talked deeply with each other.

"Yeah, that must have been it," I answered, entrenched in my thoughts, mentally excluding any other possibility. "That must've been it," I repeated to convince myself.

It would be six months before his death when I would finally learn the truth.

NORTHWESTERN UNIVERSITY EMERGENCY ROOM, CHICAGO
April 1992

Four months later, I was staring at the demon in Jonathan's body. His chest x-ray hung from a fluorescent-lit light box in front of me, looking incredibly abnormal. Fluffy white patches spread over both lungs where they should have appeared pitch-black. Pneumonia! Pneumocystis carinii pneumonia, again. The demon had a face, and I knew its name—acquired immunodeficiency syndrome—AIDS.

I had come back out to Chicago two days earlier to visit Jonathan again. I was hoping this trip would be as fun and playful as the last, but it wasn't turning out that way. Jonathan was becoming quite sick, and it was getting harder for me to deny it.

In Jonathan's apartment earlier that night, he had shouted to me from his bedroom in a panicked, wheezing voice, "Scott, can you come into the bedroom—now?!"

I quickly sprang from the couch where I had been sleeping in the living room and ran to Jonathan's side, my heart pounding.

Jon was sprawled on his bed, his face a slightly bluish, ashen color. His breaths were shallow and came at almost twice the normal rate. Every few short breaths, he would cough and wheeze heavily. "I can't breathe very well," he finally muttered. His eyes seemed to plead with me for help.

"We'll get you to the hospital right now!" I barked, helping him to his feet.

Within a few minutes, we were in his car, speeding toward Northwestern University Medical Center. Jonathan was rushed almost immediately into the emergency room, where they applied an oxygen mask, drew blood, and took the chest x-ray that I was now staring at in disbelief. Dr. Sampson, Jonathan's physician in this ER, stood next to me. Looking at the x-ray, he curtly said, "Pneumonia. Probably PCP again. We'll admit him." He crisply snapped the x-rays off of the light box and walked away without another word. I had expected Dr. Sampson to be more sensitive.

At the time of Jonathan's HIV diagnosis in 1989, his blood CD4 count was 200. The CD4 count, ranging from 600 to 1,200 in healthy individuals, is a primary way of testing how strong one's immune system is. The HIV virus directly attacks the immune system, and a lower CD4 count indicates a weakening immunity. Jonathan's count of 200 meant his immune system was critically weakened and could barely resist infection. By the time he entered Northwestern University Hospital, his CD4 level had already plummeted to 50. This demon virus was rapidly breaking down the wall of immunity that guarded him from outside invaders. No one knew how long it would be before the wall would crumble completely.

After he was admitted and given a room, I found Jon upstairs. He lay in bed, a hissing oxygen mask over his face. He inhaled the gas slowly, deliberately. His color had already returned to a more normal pinkish hue. When he saw me, that half-crooked smile of his lit up his face instantly.

"So, this is what you got me out of bed for?" I joked with a half-smile of my own.

Jon laughed, fogging up his oxygen mask. "You got to get up early in the morning to get out of bed," he quipped, referring to a line from an old Marx Brothers movie we both loved. He paused, then solemnly added, "Sorry."

"That's okay, Jon. Anyway, you'll be out of here soon. By the way, that Dr. Sampson is really no Mother Teresa!"

"Welcome to Chicago, Scott!" Jon said sarcastically, shaking his head. "There are not too many here in line for sainthood!" he said, laughing.

Jon's smile faded, and he seemed distant. In that brief moment, I could tell what he was thinking: *Why is this happening again to me? Will I make it out of the hospital this time?* His thoughts mirrored my own. It was enough that we shared thoughts; if we talked about our concerns, it would only make the nightmare more real. Deep in our hearts, Jon knew what I knew and vice versa, so talking was redundant.

"How 'bout if I get you some sushi from around the corner?" I suggested, knowing the hospital food here was probably as bad as any other.

"That sounds good," he said. "And hurry up so it stays good and cold, okay?"

I motioned with my head to the window, the frigid morning air already frosting over the pane of glass. "This is Chicago, remember? Keeping it cold is not a problem."

I left the room smiling at him, hoping for the best, but still fearing what I might return to in his precarious condition, armed with nothing more therapeutic than a handful of sushi. I wanted to believe that as his brother, his twin brother, there was more I could do for him. But it seemed there wasn't, except to just be there.

"Well, if it's warm," I heard Jon call, "I'll have to tell old Mrs. Klumpus on you, for old time's sake."

I made my way to the street, chuckling about what Jon had said. Only a twin brother could pull memories from my brain so deftly.

———

Mrs. Klumpus was a dictator and a tyrant. Unfortunately, she had also been our babysitter, twenty years earlier. Gray-haired and slightly hunched over, she must have been around seventy years old, but it was hard to tell. Jonathan, Neil, and I dreaded her teeth even more than her meanness. We mused that Mrs. Klumpus had never seen a dentist, much less a toothbrush, because her teeth were so crooked and dirty. Not one of her teeth lay in the same plane as any other, and where they did meet, they held tiny morsels of food from that day—or before. We three boys were disgusted by the sight and were convinced that she had an entire delicatessen caught between those horrible teeth. Her repugnant smile just added more misery to her visits, so it was to our advantage to keep her scowling rather than smiling. Our ultimate goal, of course, was to keep her from coming back at all. Once, we almost succeeded.

Mrs. Klumpus had come to stay with us one afternoon while our parents were out with friends. Neil, then twelve, was downstairs fixated on the television. Jonathan and I, ten, were upstairs in front of a napping Mrs. Klumpus, attempting to retaliate against her reign of terror.

We sat before her as she slept. Her mouth was slightly open, revealing just enough of those dreaded teeth to keep us motivated. Jonathan and I decided we would tie her shoes together, but we couldn't figure out how to do it without waking her up. Our precious lives seemed to depend on the little time we would have to escape after we had performed our mischievous deed.

Our plan in place, Jonathan nodded to me. We carefully placed her feet together and I quietly began to tie the laces to each other. Barely into the third knot, the dragon queen woke and snarled at us, fully baring her food-encrusted teeth. "You rotten kids!" she yelled as we raced downstairs for cover.

By the time we had run into the family room where Neil was sitting, Mrs. Klumpus had slipped out of her shoes and bolted downstairs. Her neck veins were throbbing angrily and looked as though they would burst right there. I thought her eyes would turn red and she would breathe flames.

Rather than attempt to subdue us herself, she deployed Neil as a weapon against us. Over the years, Jonathan and I had antagonized poor Neil many times, and he was all too eager to comply with Mrs. Klumpus's malevolent wishes.

"Neil!" she yelled, "Help me get them!" In 1968, corporal punishment apparently was still alive and well.

Neil jumped out of his chair and raced after us like a cat after two wild mice. But Neil was no match in speed for the twin mice! Jonathan and I raced from the house giggling, and we darted across the street. Mrs. Klumpus was still yelling, "You rotten kids!" as we ran down the sidewalk laughing, our strides identical. We ran into a narrow alleyway between two houses, the sunlight flashed, and we were gone.

> *Remember the days of moments past.*
> *They bloom like roses*
> *Then break like glass.*

I Am

> *I am the Shepherd who tends the earth,*
> *I am the Painter who colors the sky,*
> *I am the King whose command gives birth*
> *To the men that walk; to the birds that fly.*
>
> *I am the Voice that whistles the wind,*
> *I am the Hand that sweeps the sea,*
> *I am the Builder who molds the land*
> *Into mountains on high; into valleys beneath.*

I am the Flame that brightens the sun,
I set the stage for the dusk and the dawn.
I am the Planter who hoists up the trees
That race to the stars, then fall with a yawn.

I am the Guardian, the Keeper of Life,
The Tamer of the lion, the Demon in the lamb.
I am the Heaven and I am the Hell,
Yes, I am Eternal
I Am.

—Jonathan Elliot Davis

8

The Demon in the Lamb

*D*r. Davis?" I faintly heard a woman's voice calling my name. Then I heard it again, louder, and I snapped to attention. The voice belonged to the frightened mother of Jimmy, a twenty-six-year-old man I was seeing that day in the hospital's AIDS clinic. He was one of several patients there with advanced AIDS. As his doctor, I had to be professional and somewhat detached on the surface, but I felt emotionally closer to him than I should have. Neither he nor his mother would ever realize just how empathetic I truly felt. I felt as close to them as one disease could bring together complete strangers. For a few moments, I had become lost in my thoughts, until Jimmy's mother broke me out of my reverie.

Jimmy resembled Jonathan, and that made the connection even stronger for me. He had deep-set green eyes, dark brown hair with wisps of gray, and a half-crooked smile that seemed to hide some sadness. Jimmy was starting to develop an infection on his cheeks called molluscum contagiosum, a viral infection of the skin frequently seen in those with poor immune systems. It was very common in AIDS patients and difficult to treat. Jimmy's cheeks were covered with raised, mushroomlike blisters. Jonathan had just started to develop them as well. Jimmy could have been Jonathan. Yet he wasn't, and I had to remember that.

The news for Jimmy and his mother that day was not good. Despite a regimen of drugs that read like a compendium of treatment for AIDS, Jimmy's immune system was not responding. His CD4 count was below 200, meaning that his body was now wide open to much more serious infection. Short of more potent drugs to treat him with, Jimmy would likely continue to deteriorate.

"Dr. Davis, am I dying now?" Jimmy finally asked me quietly after I had completed my examination. His mother nervously stepped in closer, as though my next words would determine his fate.

"No, Jimmy, you are not dying now," I said. "Right now, you are living with AIDS. There is a big difference. New treatments are on the way soon." I always tried to be optimistic with patients if I could be. Hope is a very powerful force, especially for the terminally ill.

"So I'm doing okay right now?"

"Yeah, I'd say you are doing okay, Jimmy. We just have to watch you closely." His mother smiled for the first time. A small dose of hope to their hearts was as powerful a drug as any I could give them.

Three months later, it was July. I was feeling hopeful, too, as Jonathan and I decided to take in a weekend alone in Palm Springs. The weather that weekend in "the Springs" was miserably hot and humid—almost 110 degrees in the shade. As we drove down Highway 111 into the town of Palm Springs, steam appeared to rise from the desert floor.

Jonathan was thrilled to have that hot sun beat on his back for a change. Four months earlier, he had moved back to California mainly to escape the brutally cold weather that Chicago was so famous for. The repeated pneumonias had taken their toll on his lungs, and he could no longer tolerate breathing the frigid air. The hot California temperatures were prolonging Jonathan's life, but I thought they would kill me.

Our first stop on our weekend sojourn was, oddly, the Palm Springs Municipal Golf Course. Now, neither Jonathan nor I could by any means be mistaken for good golfers. In fact, we were hardly recognizable as players, except for the clubs in our hands and our ability to swing them somewhat. But golf was something that we could both do in mediocrity together, and that was what made it special and fun. The Twins had arrived that day at the top of the leaderboard!

The "leaderboard" on the Palm Springs Municipal Golf Course was a very lonely place that day. The scorching heat had left the golf course all but abandoned, except for a few of the most die-hard golfers.

We stood on the eighth hole tee, soaked to the skin in our T-shirts. Jonathan perched himself squarely over the ball and swung his club. The club head sank into the earth with a soft thud before sending a cloud of grass flying in all directions. The hole in the ground matched the three he had just made in similar attempts.

"Beautiful shot!" I said, shaking my head and rolling my eyes. "Step aside and I'll show you how it's done." As if my game were any more stellar!

I moved into position over the ball, bent my head down, and swung hard enough to launch the ball into a distant galaxy. The ball shot sharply right into a nearby tree and then careened backward, landing about one hundred feet *behind* us. We truly were pathetic on the golf course.

The player behind us, waiting impatiently for us to move on, was an obese hulk of a man in a perspiration-drenched undershirt and lime-green golf shorts. He didn't look anything like a pro golfer himself, but he was still bigger than us, with an attitude just as large.

Standing on the preceding seventh hole green, he shouted to us, "If you can't play, then just get the fuck off the course!" He waved his flabby arms in the direction of some distant exit.

We ignored him, and Jonathan moved toward the tee for yet another attempt at making contact with the ball.

Hulk Man yelled louder, "I said, get the fuck outta here!" This time he raised up his golf club and shook it high in the air.

Jonathan just stood there with his back toward him. I could see Jonathan's face turning beet-red with anger. Sometimes his temper could easily get the best of him. That time, it almost got the both of us. Jonathan turned back to face our nasty opponent and, without hesitation, gave him the third-finger sign, perching his golf club high up in front of his finger to exaggerate the "flip-off" gesture.

The big man suddenly took off toward us, firing off a string of expletives. Jonathan and I, both smaller and faster than he, raced down the fairway and darted left toward the cover of a dense pocket of trees. Like the eight-year-old boys who had once dashed into the dark pockets between neighborhood homes, we again disappeared into the dark thicket, still laughing. *Remember the days of moments past.*

As we raced between the trees, the man's taunts became quieter and quieter, and finally stopped. Out of breath, we broke into a small grassy clearing in the trees and collapsed onto the ground, still trying to laugh between our gasps for air. We rolled onto our backs and stared up at the blue, cloudless sky. We were thirty-two-year-old men who, for that brief moment, felt much younger.

I looked down at Jonathan's side and was suddenly reminded of the unfortunate present. A small plastic ball bulged from Jonathan's pants pocket. It fed a powerful antibiotic through a catheter and into his arm. Cytomegalovirus was the viral enemy in his bloodstream this time. The antibiotic in the plastic ball, Gancyclovir, was the only hope this time to suppress it. No cures this time, just something to stall this new virus long enough until a wave of more powerful drugs killed it off completely.

To talk to Jonathan, you would think he had all the time in the world to wait. He never talked about his illness to anyone, including me. Without as much as a single revealing word or expression, he kept it all to himself—the silent, walking wounded.

But I wanted so desperately to break through that wall of silence. I was his twin brother, for God's sake. If *anyone* should have been trying to tear down that wall between us, it should have been me.

I looked at Jonathan, who was looking up at the sky. That famous half-crooked smile of his seemed to belie the deeper fear and uncertainty that he must have really felt. I wanted to say "Jon, I understand," but really, I didn't. For the first time, in fact, I didn't know where to begin to understand.

BIG BEAR LAKE, CALIFORNIA
June 27, 1992
1:15 PM

Nestled within the sprawling San Bernardino Mountains northeast of Los Angeles, Big Bear Lake's majesty and beauty is unsurpassed. There are towering pine trees, hidden lakes and coves, and abundant wildlife. Add the warmth of an early summer breeze, and Big Bear would seem to be a nearly perfect destination for a getaway.

Jonathan, my mother, and I thought just that as we made our way to Big Bear for a long summer weekend. We all needed the relaxation desperately. I had just completed the most grueling year of medical internship and had a one-week respite before returning to my resident duties. My year had become all the more harrowing with Jonathan's ups and downs to worry about.

The last six months, though, Jonathan's health had remained surprisingly stable; the California climate and Mother's gourmet cooking skills had been good to him. Our trip to Big Bear seemed an unspoken celebration of his continued health.

"Scott, we need to do something. *You* need to do something."

Mom and I were sitting together alone in a rowboat in the middle of Big Bear Lake. There was an urgency in her voice I had not heard before.

"What do you mean, 'Do something'?" I asked. "What more can we do than his doctors are doing now?"

"I don't know. Maybe there is something they've overlooked. You're a doctor, right?"

"I am a doctor, just barely right now, but not *his* doctor. I'm his bro—"

"I know you're his brother," she said, interrupting me. She looked up toward the shore, as though looking at the lodge bedroom in the distance where Jonathan was resting. Lowering her voice, she added, "But I think he needs more right now, much more."

Of course he needed much more. Jonathan was in the eye of the hurricane, in a quiet calm now that we knew would not last. The other side would eventually catch up to him. He had begun coughing again the night before. He had felt too sick to join us on the lake and had opted instead to stay in bed for the day. Mother and I were concerned, of course, but we also needed some time to ourselves to think.

I was being drawn in—partly by my mother's insistence, partly by my own—to "do more" with Jonathan's doctors. I knew I had too little experience with this disease to truly do anything differently. I knew there was no new magical drug now that would reverse the effects of Jon's illness. But I was his *twin brother* doctor; that was the shred of hope my mother clung to.

"What about a bone marrow transplant?" she asked after a long silence. The boat rocked gently on the water. "They could use some of your bone marrow."

Several small clinical studies had been done where they had transplanted bone marrow between identical twins where one was healthy and one had AIDS. Early on in those studies, results seemed hopeful; the anemic blood counts slowly improved. But the improvements never lasted and the counts always returned to their former dismal levels.

"No, too risky," I said almost immediately. "The doctors would need to wipe out his bone marrow and immune system first, before the transplant. He's already so weak, he'd never survive an infection."

"What about—?" she began again.

"What about we just go in and see how Jon's doing first?" I interrupted. I was weary of the questions, tired of the "what abouts" and "what ifs," and just tired of being tired. I grasped the rough wooden oars and started to row the boat back toward the shore. "We'll talk about this more tomorrow," I said evasively as we rowed back in.

BIG BEAR LAKE, CALIFORNIA
June 28, 1992
4:57 AM

Mother and I never got that chance to talk. At 4:57 AM the next morning, the earth beneath the San Bernardino Mountains began to heave and convulse as a powerful earthquake ripped through the Big Bear area. Centered in Landers, just several miles away from us, the quake measured 7.3 on the Richter scale, erupting into a circular, rippling wake of destruction. The fault violently cracked into a fifty-three-mile-long rupture, devastating anything in its path.

We were sleeping in a room on the second floor of the quaint log cabin lodge when the earth shook. Jonathan, Mom, and I raced to the front doorway in darkness, barely keeping our balance as the old lodge struggled to stay together. I felt at any moment that the shaking log wall around us would give way. Jonathan and Mom, fighting their panic, struggled to free the chain latch and open the door. Finally, as the floor took its heaviest lurch forward, the latch released and we all ran out and down the stairs to the car.

Jonathan's heavy cough had now become a more labored wheeze. We knew Jonathan was getting sick again, and the fear of the earthquake had worsened his symptoms.

Somehow, driving through the chaos of earthquake-torn Big Bear, we managed to get back onto the one open mountain road leading out of town. Our escape was risky and we knew it. We were on a two-lane mountain road climbing out of Big Bear, just after a major earthquake. An aftershock could send any of the gigantic boulders above us crashing down. Jonathan needed a hospital, though, and we had no choice but to risk the drive.

Jonathan was sprawled across the backseat, breathing heavily, his face ashen from illness and fear. "Take some slow breaths, Jon. You'll be okay," I tried to reassure him, not really believing that myself.

We all jumped in our seats as several small stones pelted the car from the cliff above us. Then my mother veered the car sharply to the right, avoiding a small landslide of rocks that had collected in the road.

"Now I *really* don't feel so good," Jon said sarcastically. Even when he was miserable, he always managed to inject humor into a stressful moment.

By the time we finally arrived at Sherman Oaks Hospital two hours later, Jonathan was seriously ill. In the emergency room his doctor explained to us that the complication this time was a very aggressive pancreatitis. The cytomegalovirus was back again in his body with a vengeance. This time it had set its sights on his liver and pancreas.

When he was finally brought into the intensive care unit (ICU), his body temperature had soared to a critical 106 degrees, which was literally life threatening. In place of a usual warm saline solution, his ICU nurse immediately started a fast intravenous drip of ice-cold solution to lower his body temperature. Potent "big gun" antibiotics were infused into his IV lines to fight off secondary bacterial infections.

Jonathan had rapidly become dehydrated and delirious. The toxic effects of the infection were taking their toll on his already weakened body.

An hour later, we sat in the ICU waiting room just outside the unit. I sat in silence, nervously tapping my fingertips together, thinking. With all of my medical knowledge, I understood that Jonathan was seriously ill this time. AIDS, at this time of relatively poor treatment for it, was aggressive and usually fatal.

Yet my brother had proven himself to be equally resilient in fighting the unavoidable complications of AIDS. I still did not understand what he thought or even how he managed to be so stoic in this personal war of his. But this sailor could take a hit and still keep moving forward. Jonathan never complained and never spoke a word to me about his illness. His quiet courage taught me a lesson in keeping the blind faith.

At around 6:00 PM, Jonathan's physician, Dr. Gottlieb, walked into the waiting room. "Well," he said, "this episode has really hit him pretty hard. The liver and pancreas are very inflamed with lots of angry fluid around them." I bit down on my quivering lip, anticipating the worse news to come. "But," Dr. Gottlieb continued, "Jonathan's fever is coming down, his blood pressure is improving, and—you know what he just said to me?"

"What?" my mother asked.

"He said, 'If this thing is trying to kill me, it'll have to do a much better job than this!'" We all laughed, and it felt good. "Knowing Jonathan, with a line like that, chances are good he'll be stickin' around for a while. You can go in and see him if you'd like."

Five days later, a weakened but buoyant Jonathan left the hospital. Two months later, he again returned. His illness was relentless.

Ironically, our ill-fated trip to Big Bear Lake in June 1992 seemed like a metaphor for the final turbulent year of Jonathan's life. His trips to the hospital became more frequent, and his precious periods of relative health became shorter.

With each day that Jonathan became sicker, I became less and less concerned with exactly *how* he had contracted his illness. We assumed it had been when he had his transfusion, but we didn't really know for sure. Honestly, I had my doubts he had gotten it that way, but I never asked him about it. If Jonathan had acquired the HIV infection from a homosexual relationship, I would not have felt any differently about him. I loved him for who he was and for the brotherhood we had. But

I also knew that Jonathan could be very guarded, even secretive, with his personal life. At the risk of not knowing the details of "how," I respected his privacy and didn't ask. There were things about my twin brother I still did not really know, and with less time to find out more about him, this once-burning question of "How?" took a much lower priority in my mind. Jonathan and I never talked about who we were to each other. I did not want to tamper with that precious balance in our relationship now. He had proven himself to be a resilient warrior. I thought I still had plenty of time to get to know him better.

9

The Heaven and the Hell

Two Years After Jonathan's Death

*A*re you sleeping well, Scott?" Dr. Miota asked me that afternoon. *Sure I am,* I thought, as I lay awake in my darkened bedroom that evening. I didn't want to spend one more night awake, tangled in a web of unpleasant memories, but here I was again, trying to remember Jonathan as a healthy, laughing boy instead of a frail, sick man. I tried to imagine how life might have been different if his illness had not come between us, but I could only recall how things had truly unfolded.

That afternoon I had nodded and said, "Yes, Dr. Miota, I'm sleeping well," and it had not been a lie. I *had* been sleeping well, but only because of the strong sedative, Ambien, that I had used night after night, week after week, and month after month since Jonathan's death.

During the day, I was a busy new doctor in a growing internal medicine practice. I saw patients all day long without breaks so I would have no time left to think about Jonathan. With his death still as fresh in my mind as a raw, festering wound, I had no desire to.

But at night, it was different. Alone in my quiet bedroom, there were no patients to distract me. There was nothing to keep me from climbing back into my own head and living Jonathan's life again and again. The lonely nights had wretched memories in store for me, and I refused to simply give in to them.

Many times lying in bed at night I could feel a presence in my room, as though someone were watching me. The sensation was strange, the room dark and empty, with an aura around me that made me feel as if I were not alone. One night when I was watching television, I restlessly changed the channels with the remote, and the name "Jonathan" was broadcast from every channel. While one mention of his name would have seemed merely a coincidence, I heard his name spoken on several different channels, one after another. I didn't know if this was my mind playing tricks on me or truly some paranormal presence of Jonathan.

I glanced again at the clock on my nightstand. It was 11:30. The sedative I had taken ten minutes before was beginning to take effect, and I gratefully accepted the first happy memory that came to mind.

"Where are the boys?" Nana Sally yelled. "Sheila, where are the boys?" She paused, then screamed, "Damn it, no one ever listens to Nana Sally. Why should they? She *never* has anything worth listening to anyway. Damn it!" She could be so sarcastic it was funny.

The third time Nana screamed, "Where are the boys?" young Jonathan and I flew past her like speeding comets. She twirled around to grab us, but we were too fast for her; we were too fast for anyone! This was the same Nana Sally who had fainted from joy upon hearing of our births. Now she often claimed to be traumatized by our very existence.

We shot outside into the backyard through the narrowest opening in the sliding glass door. As we disappeared, giggling, we were privy to another barrage of expletives from Nana Sally that no child should be allowed to hear. But we were like the crowned princes of boyhood antics, and hearing Nana Sally scream was the absolute jewel in the crown.

Love comes in many forms; Nana Sally's love had a very rough, abrasive quality to it. Some grandparents shower their grandchildren with hugs and kisses, praise and affection, but Nana hollered and complained to show how much she loved us, and we all knew it.

Upon seeing that we could not be controlled, Nana marched into the entrance foyer and up the stairs, scowling and shaking her head. "No one ever listens to Nana! No one!" she spat. She reached the landing at the top of the stairs, raised her hands up melodramatically, and shouted, "My God, I'm so upset I must be having a heart attack!"

When hearing this, Nat, her husband—"Papa Nat" to Jon, Neil, and I—walked in from the kitchen yelling, "Sally, you're not having a heart attack, you're having an insanity streak!" Papa Nat was used to Nana.

With that, Nana stormed into her room. "I'd rather be mean than sorry!" she hollered back, her voice trailing off into the bedroom.

I smiled as I lay there in my bed, the sedative pulling me deeper and deeper away from reality. The images in my mind softened and grew hazy. I embraced the artificial peace that blanketed me.

What I've Known

There is a space into which that I've known,
Confining myself to a solace and peace.
Into there I emerge undaunted, profound,
Into where but this silence welcomes my keep.

By its nature, it holds my grip from the light,
Showing no view within the black of my space.
Beyond it: passion, promise, and greed.
But here, no scars of social debase.

For here, I retreat into the crypt of my soul,
A physical gorge that beats with my pulse.
Not locked within, for here is my truth.
And in the depth of my being, I cry at its false.

Yes, there is a space to where I can go.
But though tragic and grateful and never still awed,
Does this silence so painful hinder my reach
To the light of Dear God, from this darkness so flawed?

—Jonathan Elliot Davis

10

I Am Eternal, I Am

*T*he more I tried to ignore the truth, the more it bore into me. In time, my pain reached out from my mind and memories and took hold of my physical being.

First, I had a sudden pain in my upper stomach area. Within minutes, it had spread to the right side of my abdomen, centered over my liver. The pain was intense and felt like someone was wringing and squeezing the area like a sponge. The pressure was so bad that any movement seemed almost impossible.

Jonathan had suffered through intense abdominal pain, too. For nearly two years, until his death, he was plagued by repeated bouts of abdominal pain. The viral culprit, cytomegalovirus, found my brother to be a perfect host time and time again. First it attacked his pancreas and liver, sending him to the hospital and nearly taking his life.

Then repeated invasions of his colon, called colitis, sent him running back to his doctor for stronger and stronger pain-killers. It was another flare-up of colitis that brought him back to the hospital—for the final time.

My abdominal pain felt like a vise that slowly and method-ically gripped and relaxed its hold on me. As soon as the grip would loosen a bit, I would exhale, savoring the momentary relief. But just as quickly, the pain would return again. Only morphine in my veins could bring relief that lasted more than a few seconds.

Jonathan indeed had endured years of this distress. This time, however, it was different: Jonathan had been dead for two years.

The pain was all mine.

"Now just relax, Scott. The pain will be gone in just a second."

"Not soon enough," I managed to squeak, as the operating room anesthesiologist pushed the syringe plunger and released a dose of morphine into my arm.

She was right. Within seconds, the morphine found its tar-get in my brain and the tight constriction in my gut began to relax. The rest of my tired body soon followed, and I began to slowly drift into a drug-induced haze. As I lay on the operat-ing room table, awaiting the final anesthetic descent into sleep, I remembered the very reason I was here. On one of the sterile metal trays next to me lay a small steel disk about the size of a hockey puck. A thin plastic catheter about one foot long snaked out from the side of the disk. This disk was a state-of-the-art pain control device—a pump that would be surgically implanted in my abdomen to deliver a continuous flow of morphine. Completely programmable by a computer from outside my body, it would deliver precise bursts of morphine to my brain and spinal cord. The small implanted catheter attached to the pump would feed the drug directly onto nerve roots in my spinal cord and into the fluid bathing my brain. Any intense abdominal pain I suffered would be completely eradicated on contact.

"Don't worry," Dr. Praeger, my pain specialist, had said to me one week earlier in his office. "It's a very safe device. It gives very low doses of morphine. I got pilots and judges walking around with these. Don't even worry about getting addicted to this thing. Besides, you're a responsible doctor and a great candidate for this pump. You know better." He laughed and shook his head as though he were stating the obvious.

At that moment, I knew that my responsibility and judgment would not fare well against a powerful drug like morphine. I *did* know better, but I also knew that whatever addiction I had before the pump went in would be fired up like rocket fuel once the morphine took hold. But I was tired of the pain, wherever it was coming from. Addiction almost seemed a welcome release.

"We're ready to begin, Scott," Dr. Praeger said. He injected a more potent anesthetic called Propofol into my intravenous line. Within seconds I was drifting into a pleasant unconsciousness, away from reality again. The dream was always the same.

A Toasting of Conspirators

"Good evening, friends," the old man spoke,
"I toast you with this wine,
Which—sad but true—I shall consume
And end this life of mine."

"You are a fool!" Time cried out,
"To drink that wicked brew,
And die before the friends you trust
When enemies you have few."

"Yes, you are right," the old man frowned,
"My trust had never tired,
But great dreams that I once sacrificed—"

"Great dreams?" the Past inquired,
"Ah, scattered dreams you were,
For a man whose life lay in a failing plane,
Such dreams could not occur."

"Then pity not his ignorance," said Honor with a smile,
"Since the old man's sense of dignity
Spans a many mile."

"Conspirators you are!" the old man cried,
"Is this your mere betrayal?
Does Time just lead to Death and Honor, disgrace?
What injustice here prevails?"

"So I depart," the old man sighed,
"Betrayed by a conscience which I gave birth,
Never more to count life's grandest hours
But die by this hand that held no worth!"

"Then good night," said Honor,
With one final breath.
"Farewell," whispered Life.
"Have some wine," smiled Death.

—Jonathan Elliot Davis

11

"Farewell,"
Whispered Life

*W*e're going to give you some anesthetic, Scott, and then you'll be asleep," Dr. Cotton said gently. One year before Dr. Praeger would plant the morphine pump inside me and wipe out my chronic pain, Dr. Cotton had attempted to find its elusive cause.

Many doctors had tried. I had had lots of x-rays, CAT scans, and MRIs, but they had all been normal. I had tried herbal remedies, psychotherapy, and acupuncture. Nothing worked. One physician removed my gallbladder, but my pain persisted. Three months after that, another doctor explored my biliary and pancreatic ducts with an invasive procedure called ERCP, but he found nothing as well. With no answer and no relief, I was referred to Dr. Cotton, an internationally known gastroenterologist who specialized in the liver and pancreas. When other doctors could not end a patient's pain or find its cause, they called Dr. Cotton. He was like Red Adair, the famous firefighter, except the fires he put out burned in the gastrointestinal tract.

By the time I was finally positioned onto Dr. Cotton's operating room table, I was heavily addicted to narcotics and sleeping pills. Narcotics quelled my physical and emotional pain by day, and sleeping pills by night. It was a vicious cycle. Each pill I took reinforced my need and desire to take the next. Each doctor who examined me, probed me, or cut into me hoped to be the one to reveal the source of my pain. But one by one, they failed, and gave me painkillers as a consolation prize.

Somehow, though, I knew that this unremitting pain lay far deeper than any knife or endoscope could reach. I knew that no matter how much tissue was removed from my body or how many holes were made to relieve internal pressure, the pain would continue. Jonathan's death had created a cavernous void inside of me that could not simply be filled. Nothing could fill that space like he had. My pain was a constant reminder of that void, so when I was given the chance to deaden it, I jumped for it.

Several hours after Dr. Cotton had completed his own endoscopic exam, he spoke with me in my hospital room. Shaking his head, he explained, "I couldn't find anything wrong, Scott, nothing to explain what's causing all this pain. You got any ideas?" He chuckled gently.

"No ideas," I said, "but there has to be something physically wrong!" I had to keep those pain meds coming. It was my only hope against having to deal with where the pain was really coming from.

Dr. Cotton shrugged his shoulders, at a loss for an answer.

"I'd like to refer you to a pain specialist at UCLA, a Dr. Praeger, who might be able to help. I'll call him, tell him what's going on, and that you'll be contacting him for an appointment. Until then, here's something else for the pain." He handed me a written prescription for Percocet, a narcotic even stronger than I had been taking.

I was worried: just one more doctor, one more prescription, with no one thinking to look any deeper than my physical body. Yet the addict inside me was thrilled.

Over the next year Dr. Praeger, the pain specialist, did his job well. He continued to mask my pain with repeated prescriptions of more and more potent narcotics. I simply justified to myself that since I had pain, I was entitled to take them. Unfortunately, with addiction comes a sense of entitlement that feeds upon itself—like a growing cancer that ultimately robs its own blood supply. I, in turn, was an addict who had become both provider and thief.

Desperate to give me some definitive pain control, Dr. Praeger finally implanted the morphine pump inside me.

As part of the protocol, Dr. Praeger referred me to Dr. Miota, a psychiatrist specializing in addiction treatment. Her job was to see to it that I wouldn't develop a runaway drug problem while being continuously pumped full of morphine. But by that time, I already had.

SHERMAN OAKS MEDICAL CENTER
Intensive Care Unit
July 23, 1993
12:30 PM

The waiting room adjacent to Jonathan's room in the intensive care unit was very quiet. One hour before, I had quickly returned to the hospital after our friend, Pat, had summoned me back.

"You have to come back to the hospital now," she had said urgently. "Jonathan has taken a turn for the worse."

On returning to the hospital, I found my mother, Pat, and friend Sandie sitting nervously in the waiting room. They were alone, and the room was uncomfortably heavy with tension.

"Where's Dad?" I asked my mother.

"He's in Jonathan's room. Dad wanted to be alone with him for a minute."

"Alone?" I asked fearfully. My first thought was that Jonathan had died, and I hadn't been there with him. My heart began to race, and I started to quickly walk out toward Jonathan's room.

"No," Mom said quickly, knowing what I was thinking. "Jon's stable right now. Dad just needed a few minutes by himself."

I took a deep breath. Jonathan was stable. This was good news for the moment. I began to sit down, but then Dad appeared at the door. He looked as though he had aged years since I had seen him just an hour before. His face and shoulders were sunken down, and his reddened, tear-filled eyes spoke before he did.

"I think we're losing Jonathan," he choked.

I opened my eyes and I was safely back in Dr. Miota's office. The good doctor had been guiding me on a journey in my mind, back to the day of Jonathan's death. But I had stopped myself. I could not, even in my mind, walk from the hospital waiting room and into Jonathan's room as I had that day. Not yet.

Dr. Miota was staring down her nose at me from her chair. I had come to expect her gentle prodding by now, but it was still uncomfortable. She wanted to lead me down this painful memory lane as easily as if it were some peaceful garden path. But I was in no mood to be picking flowers.

"Well, here we are again, Scott," she said, flipping her hands up in mock frustration. "Right back where we always seem to stop."

"What do you mean?" I shot back.

"You know what I mean. You just don't want to go back into that room."

"That's because there's nothing to talk about, Dr. Miota."

She just sat there with her head tilted. I knew she saw me hitting another wall.

Then she said quietly, "Scott, what happened in that room that you don't want to talk about?"

I was beginning to feel nauseated and uncomfortable, and Dr. Miota could see it. She knew that her psychiatric probe had twisted me into some dark, forbidden corner. Determined to tease out something incredibly sensitive, she waited for my reply.

I closed my eyes and smiled. In my mind I began once again to walk down some happier garden path toward a distant childhood memory, one that would take me far away from reality, back to a less threatening time.

Dr. Miota sighed. She knew she had lost me again.

The familiar scene I disappeared into was a crowded restaurant, packed to the walls with customers and waiters moving nonstop. In the center of the single large room, we sat around a circular table—my mother, father, Nana Sally and Papa Nat, and Jon, Neil, and I. Earlier that afternoon had been when Papa Nat had accused Nana Sally of having an "insanity streak," not a heart attack, as she had claimed.

I think my parents had hoped to ease the tension between them with a relaxing family dinner, but Nana Sally was never one to quickly give up on a good resentment. She decided, instead, to take her bitter mood to dinner with us that night.

"Excuse me, may I have a drink?" she called to a waiter as he hurried by. Nana's thin voice was almost engulfed by the loud chatter around her, and he didn't hear her.

Another waiter swept by the table. "Oh, excuse me," Nana said more loudly, "May I please get a drink!" Her high-pitched request again went unheard or ignored.

Nana Sally was now furious. She had been ignored long enough. She raised her arms and shook them in the air as though she were parting the Red Sea, shrieking, "May I have a drink? Just one damn drink! What do I have to do, get on my knees and beg for a drink?"

The waiter froze, as did all of the restaurant patrons within shouting distance of our table. Nana Sally looked down at all of us and shook her head as though trying to shake off the looks of embarrassment on our faces. "I'd just rather be mean than sorry," she repeated quietly for the rest of the dinner.

12

"Have Some Wine," Smiled Death

So tell me about that last day on the job, Scott."

Last day on the job, I thought. *What a gentle way Dr. Miota had of saying, "The worst day of my life." You mean the day I got fired and tossed out of the office, right?*

I really did not want to even go there. But I sighed and followed her lead back into the questioning.

"The last night of my use turned into the last day."

She looked at me, puzzled. "What do you mean?"

I sat there and once again tried to think back to a happier time, a more comforting place in my childhood, a softer memory to keep me from going where I did not want to go.

Dr. Miota knew where I was headed by the blank look on my face. "Don't go there, Scott. Just stay with me and tell me what happened."

Just the thought of going back to that final day began

stirring up emotions. "It might be better not to talk about it," I said.

Dr. Miota stared at me with her caring but probing look. "It might feel worse not to. You know, there's something that's troubling me, Scott."

"Like what?"

"Well, there's something that you just don't want to talk about. Every time I try to move forward with you, you want to move back. Your childhood and your family, well, seem a pretty comfortable place for you to be—in your own head."

Damn, she was good. Too good!

"There's a problem with that?" I asked.

She looked at me and dropped her chin as if to say, "You know there's a problem with that."

I knew there was a problem with that, too, but it was just too painful to go back there. So I started speaking about the last night of my drug use. It was painful, but not nearly as bad as where Dr. Miota wanted me to go. It was painful to think and talk about it, but it had been worse to live through.

That night, I finally returned home from work to the small apartment my wife, Rebecca, and I rented. Rebecca knew I was getting and using prescription drugs on top of the morphine that was still flowing through me. She knew I was lying about them and certainly knew I was hiding them. The beast of a disease called addiction just kept me doing it.

I had taken Rebecca's car to work that day. I arrived back home after work and pulled her car into the parking space next to mine. She said she had taken my car to get it washed and detailed, but she actually had searched every inch of it for drugs. And she had found them.

I reached into my car and pulled the cover off the fuse box. I expected to find the string attached to the bagful of Ambien sleeping pills lowered into the fuse box, where I had hidden them. Instead, I found nothing.

I panicked. I imagined she had found them and thrown them out, and was now waiting to verbally attack me when I walked in. I wanted to just drive away, find an all-night pharmacy, and write myself one more prescription. Walk upstairs or drive away? I was trapped either way.

My mind shot back to when Rebecca had found a stash of my Ambien sleeping pills that I had hidden in a shoe in our bedroom closet. As I came through the front door that day, I watched her angrily walk down the stairs, her knuckles clenched white around the pills. She marched to the back of the apartment, opened the back door and launched the pills into the patio garden. Without a word, she brushed by me as she stomped back upstairs and slammed the bedroom door closed.

"You'll feel so much better, Scott."

The addict inside me took hold. I ran into the garden and feverishly began collecting the scattered pills I desperately needed. I intensely searched under every leaf, though I could only find a few of the many tiny pills she had hurled. As I walked back into the house, I caught a glimpse of Rebecca staring out at me from the upstairs bedroom window. She was crying, with a look of pain and despair. I had seen that look before.

Night after night she lay next to me in our bedroom, hurt and angry over my relentless drug use. I would always choose my "little white mistress pill" as she called it, abandoning her in favor of my escape from reality when I took the pill and fell asleep fast.

I saw that look before the many times we drove together, with a tension-filled silence thick between us.

I saw that look in countless places, many of those memories now blurred by the chronic effect of those drugs that hinder me from recalling them. Addicted and self-absorbed, I emotionally alienated myself from the marriage and did nothing to change that look on her face.

"You'll feel so much better, Scott," the addict inside urged me to pop my next sedating dose.

I walked upstairs to the apartment and went in. I could see Rebecca sleeping soundly in the bedroom. I had never seen her sleep so peacefully before. With my sleeping pills gone, I reasoned she must have taken them herself. Was she trying to escape from the harsh reality of living with an addict, as I tried to escape from my own reality with pills? Even in my addicted state, I knew she must have felt miserable watching us grow further apart. I deeply loved her, but the drugs were so easily anesthetizing my emotions toward her.

"Scott, find those pills and take them. You'll feel so much better," taunted my inner addict voice.

I collapsed on the couch in the living room, exhausted. My head began to swirl. I was overwhelmed with guilt, shame, and fear for what I had led her to do. My addiction was destroying me. It was destroying Rebecca. I put my head in my hands and cried.

"Then Good night," said Honor,
With one final breath,
"Farewell," whispered Life.
"Have some wine," smiled Death.

I must have sat there and cried for no more than a minute when a voice in my head began to talk to me.

"Those pills may still be in the car, Scott," the voice echoed, teasing me. *"Rebecca never found them and you just misplaced them in there. You know you need them. Go find them before she wakes up."*

The urge to find them and take them once again began to grip me like a cold vice. Once it clamped down, it was unshakable.

I left the apartment and ran down the stairs back to the car. I drove out of the parking lot and crossed the street into a large vacant supermarket parking lot. I felt a cold sweat of anticipation starting on my forehead. I could almost taste the pills in my mouth.

I pulled into a darkened corner of the parking lot, pulled a flashlight from my glove box, and, in a frenzy, began to rip off the dashboard. I didn't care that the car was leased. I didn't care that I was endangering myself, alone in a dark, empty lot. I just needed those pills!

With the dashboard nearly completely off its mountings, I searched every nook and cranny desperately.

Nothing.

I pounded on the steering wheel and then grabbed it tightly as though it were the only thing holding me down. I was out of control. I knew that. I just couldn't stop!

I looked across the lot to the entrance of the Sav-On pharmacy. It was closed for the night. This pharmacy was one of my "havens" where I had gotten many prescriptions. I didn't want to take a chance at another pharmacy so late at night. I might get caught.

I knew what I had to do. The next morning I would go to the pharmacy near my office. I would arm myself with another one of many prescriptions I had written for myself. "Michael Milken" was the name I would use—again. I would get a small quantity, thirty or forty, no refills, nothing to set off any "red alerts" behind the counter. I would intentionally leave my identification in the car, so if the pharmacist asked for it, I would truthfully have none and I would simply walk out.

I had repeated this scenario week after week, month after month. One more time would be easy—just another prescription for Ambien sleeping pills or Vicodin narcotics—anything to dull the pain or keep the demons out of my head was a blessing.

But that night I would have nothing. I knew it would be a sleepless night, a drug-deficient insomnia. I knew the demons inside my head were just waiting for me to turn out the lights and start thinking. They would conjure up thoughts of Jonathan, of the years we'd lost together. They might even take me to that one place that I feared the most—the hour before Jonathan's death. It would be a long night.

13

Silence That
Welcomes My Keep

*T*hat long, sleepless night turned into the final day. My workday in the medical office as an internist passed uneventfully. For six months, I had been seeing patients in Santa Clarita, California, for a large managed-care company. Life for me was the daily grind of ten-minute appointments, thirty times a day, every day.

The pace of such an office-based HMO practice was supercharged and stressful, and too frenetic for some doctors; many who joined the group would soon leave in search of more relaxed work environments. Others who stayed eased their daily tensions with a longer lunch, a workout at a nearby gym in the afternoon, or an evening out after work. I had my own stress-relief plan—and it was killing me!

The morphine pump fed me continuously, but even that wasn't enough. On that day, at 3:00 PM—as I did every day—

I quietly went into one of the restrooms in the office and locked the door. As usual at this time, my leg muscles were beginning to cramp up and spasm, as the dose of narcotics I had taken earlier began to wear off. Within a minute, the spasms intensified to where walking became very difficult. I sat down on the toilet, fished several more Vicodin tablets from my pocket, and swallowed them. I knew it would take nearly an hour for the pills to take effect, but I began to relax, just knowing I had taken them.

As I walked back into my office, the clinic director, Dr. Hoffman, poked his head in the door.

"Scott, I need to see you in my office—now," he said sharply. Dr. Hoffman usually was very jovial, but this time he sounded very serious. I couldn't imagine what was up.

I walked into his office and also found our assistant director, Dr. Michael Burton, sitting in the office, looking concerned. I sat down and Dr. Hoffman spoke. "Scott, I'm waiting for a fax to come through now that I'd like you to explain to me." He looked at me sternly, as though he wanted me to speak rather than wait for the fax. I stayed silent as my pulse quickened.

"This fax," he continued, "is a copy of a prescription with your signature. The prescription was brought into a pharmacy this morning. According to the pharmacist, you fit the description of the person delivering it, and—oh, here comes the fax now."

A copy of a written prescription clicked quickly out of his fax machine. Dr. Hoffman pulled it out and held it in front of me. It was the prescription I had written to myself that morning. "Michael Milken is the patient," he said. I felt my skin turn ashen. "Scott, we have no record that this patient even exists."

Terrified, I could not speak. The pharmacist had figured out that it was a bogus prescription. My heart raced. I feared that at any moment a drug enforcement agent would walk into the office and arrest me.

"Did you write this to yourself, Scott?" Dr. Hoffman asked quietly.

My addicted brain went into defense mode. "Of course not," I said defiantly.

"Scott, one more time, did you write this?" Dr. Hoffman asked, though he knew the truth.

Again I held my ground. "No," I said.

"Then we will have no choice but to fully investigate this, and you'll be suspended without pay while we do it."

The word *investigate* sounded horrible. It conjured up images of serious people in dark suits poring over pharmacy records, uncovering dozens of narcotic and tranquilizer pre-scriptions I had written to feed my own addiction. What had started out as an easy way to hide my emotions and escape my grief had grown into an uncontrollable monster. Pharmacies across the city would be the site of *investigations* where the monster had been. I would, at the very least, lose my medical license. I could even go to jail. I didn't like the odds at all.

"Yes, I wrote the prescription," I finally said quietly, my eyes welling up.

Several incredibly long seconds passed, then Dr. Hoffman simply said gently, "You're terminated from this employment. I'll need your badge now. I'll need your key card. We'll be speaking to you later. We're done here."

I surrendered the badge and card and stood up to leave. I was relieved to walk out on my own rather than be dragged out by authorities. I reached for the doorknob.

"Scott," Dr. Hoffman said quietly, "Get some help."

As I walked out, I wondered how I would get my drugs. The potent morphine was still coursing through my brain. The addict monster inside me was still alive and well and looking for his next fix. Dr. Hoffman was right—I needed help.

14

To the Light of Dear God

*H*is name was Jim. He had no last name, at least none that Jonathan would readily admit to. He was just Jim.

In 1979, when my twin brother was accepted by the U.S. Coast Guard to travel around the world, he was a model Sea Cadet. His young passion for the sea and for taking direction well from his commanders quickly earned their respect. When the Coast Guard cutter left San Diego for a world cruise, Jonathan was on board. Jim was with him.

Jim was the only other Sea Cadet allowed to participate in this adventure. When the cutter left its port, with hundreds of family and friends waving good-bye, Jonathan and Jim were its two novice sailors among one hundred crewmen. The day of their departure, I watched Jonathan beaming with pride from the deck, waving happily as the boat slipped away from its berth and into the calm harbor channel.

At some time during the six-month voyage, Jonathan and Jim became more than just fellow shipmates. They became lovers. "It only happened once," Jonathan reluctantly revealed to my mother. Six months before Jonathan's death, they sat alone in my mother's car in a supermarket parking lot, a heavy rain beating against the windshield.

"Jim and I were together one night, that's all," Jonathan confessed with his head down. I imagine he was waiting for a harsh rebuke from our mother, but the reprimand he feared never came. There was only a tense silence, followed by a long, quiet sigh from our mother. She loved her son dearly, and she was grateful to hear the truth. "I think that's how it happened, how I—I got infected," he had finally admitted to her.

AIDS can take up to ten years to fully develop, following the initial infection. Jonathan was diagnosed with AIDS ten years after this encounter with Jim. It is indeed likely this was how he acquired his disease.

Jonathan was a very private man, not one to readily provide details of anything. Being his twin, I thought I knew him well simply because I *was* his twin. I never asked for details about his private life because I never really thought I needed them. But I had never considered the possibility that Jonathan would keep anything important from me. It must have been hard for him to carry around such a secret for so long.

15

Darkness So Flawed

SPRINGBROOK NORTHWEST
September 1999

*S*cott, wake up. It's time to get moving!" A fist gently punched at my ribs. I didn't open my eyes or move, trying to pretend I wasn't really where I was.

"Get up, little Scotty," my roommate Carl repeated. "You're in treatment now, and it's time to get treated—again!" He laughed.

It was true. I groaned and pulled the covers over my head.

Springbrook Northwest was the treatment center. Located almost thirty miles south of Portland, Oregon, Springbrook was one of the primary centers in the country devoted to treating addictions. Within three weeks after my final meeting with Dr. Hoffman, the "help" he had suggested I get—with intense pressure from my wife to get help—evolved into a plane trip

to Oregon. I was to begin treatment for my addiction to opiates and sedatives or be assured of soon losing my medical
license. I might also be *investigated*. Neither option seemed
very palatable.

But I had an ace up my sleeve.

The staff at Springbrook had allowed me to keep the morphine pump in place while I began treatment. They reasoned
that I was legitimately being treated for chronic pain, albeit
with a highly addictive drug. I would start the treatment
process and then be encouraged to get rid of the pump.

Of course, they were trying to reason with someone who
was still continuously loaded on morphine. Flying high on
morphine, I still thought I could possibly get out of treatment
for addiction. After all, I had been allowed to enter the drug
treatment program still tethered to morphine; perhaps they
saw me simply as a chronic pain patient, not a real drug addict.
I had been at Springbrook for two weeks when I put that rea-
soning to the test.

I was taking what is called the First Step in recovery, where
you begin to admit how powerless and unmanageable your life
has become around drugs. The process is usually a painful one.
The addict or alcoholic recounts the cancerous effect of his
disease on his family, his job, his social life, and anything else
that stood in the way of using drugs. Full-blown addictions
take many casualties, not just the user.

But I wasn't an addict, I reasoned. I figured I would tell my
story to the therapy group, they would see I was not an addict,
and they would let me go.

That morning I found myself seated in a circle of chairs in
a small group room at Springbrook. The morphine pump

whirred softly in my belly as it dispersed another dose. "Why don't you start, Scott?" our counselor, Manny, urged.

Twelve male addict and alcoholic patients stared back at me. Most of them leaned forward in their chairs, anxious for me to begin. I knew they were just waiting for me to piece together my story—to confirm what I alone did not believe—that I was an addict in need of treatment.

Ryan was the only one not leaning forward, obviously disinterested. He sat across from me, eyes closed, arms tight across his chest. Ryan resented me and I knew it, as did everyone else. Ryan was an opiate addict, still bitterly craving heroin after two weeks in treatment. He was not angry with me—we had barely spoken three words since I was admitted. He resented the morphine pump that he couldn't have. Whenever the subject of my pump would arise in group, Ryan just closed his eyes, shook his head, and said, "Ah, fuck it!" When Ryan started craving drugs, his vocabulary could become quite limited.

Generally, a full, detailed account of a patient's drug-addicted story might take thirty minutes or longer, but I was finished with my entire First Step in ten minutes. The disbelief of my peers couldn't have been more obvious.

Not surprisingly, Ryan was the first to speak out.

"What the fuck just came out of your mouth, Davis?" he shot at me, seeming to take some pleasure in venting some of his anger.

"What do you mean?" I asked. The naïveté of my response heated the disbelief in the room even more.

"What I mean is—" I started.

"What he means is . . ." Tony, another addict, interrupted, "is that you did the best damn job of editing I ever heard. That

First Step not only didn't crack the ice of what happened in your life, it didn't even go near it. There has to be a whole lot more that you didn't want to talk about, Scott!"

From across the room, Peter spoke up. "You know, I feel like there's a big, deep, dark well in front of you that you don't even want to go near."

There is a space to where I can go. My skin crawled and I felt my heart race. It *was* like a well I kept trying to sidestep—like the mouth of that dark culvert Jonathan had fallen into as a child. The darkness of that tunnel was too foreboding for me to look at to help him. This felt the same.

With one soft-spoken remark, Peter had chipped away a piece around me. I swallowed hard and fought back a tear. I hoped my peers would stop and just move on to someone else's sharing for the morning group. *Does this silence so painful hinder my reach . . .*

Instead, the counselor, Manny, continued, "Scott, there's a lot more to talk about here, isn't there?" I shrugged my shoulders and lowered my head, fighting back the tears and the pain. I didn't want to go anywhere near the well.

"No, there's nothing else, Manny." I knew that Manny knew differently. *To the light of Dear God, from this darkness so flawed?*

"Then let's take a ten-minute break," Manny said with a soft, frustrated sigh.

As I walked to the door with the others, Manny stopped me, obviously not satisfied with the little information I had shared.

"Hey, Scott, whatever happened to that shrink you were seeing, that Dr.—"

"Dr. Miota?"

"Yeah, Dr. Miota. You were seeing her for a while, it sounds like. Then she was, like, gone. What happened?"

"I don't know, Manny." *I did know.* "I guess she was just getting too close," I breathed out slowly. I had not wanted to say that. It just slipped out.

"Too close to what?" Now Manny was getting too close.

I hesitated for a few seconds, and then said with my eyes lowered, "Too close to the truth."

As soon as I said that, I knew I was in trouble. I had opened a Pandora's box of deep secrets. Manny loved to open boxes of secrets!

At the break, the other patients walked off toward the kitchen area in the hall for coffee. Normally, I would have joined them for a caffeine boost and some light conversation. Today, I was feeling anything but sociable.

I turned left out of the meeting room and quickly walked down the opposite hallway to my bedroom. I went in, closed the door, and sat down on the bed. My hands were shaking so hard that I held them together to keep them steady. I closed my eyes tightly to keep the dam of tears from bursting. Why wouldn't they just leave me alone?

16

Retreat into the Crypt
of My Soul

I walked back into the group room feeling tense and confined, like a matador returning to face the bull in round two of the bullfight.

When Ryan saw me, he closed his eyes and pinched the bridge of his nose. I knew he was disgusted with my less-than-revealing performance. It wouldn't have taken much for him to feel that way about me, although I knew the others felt the same way.

"Scott, I want you to do something," Manny said to me when everyone was finally seated. Again, they all leaned forward in anticipation. This time, even Ryan leaned in to listen.

"I want you to close your eyes." I closed my eyes.

"Now I want you to see with your mind—I want you to see that deep well in front of you." He was using Peter's deep, dark well analogy.

I knew where Manny was going with this one. I didn't like it at all.

"Now take a step or two toward the well," he urged me. One could have heard a feather drop on the floor in that room.

I shook my head. "No, Manny, I really don't want to do that," my voice cracking slightly.

"Just try it, slowly, just to the edge now." His tone was soft but unyielding, as though he was pushing from behind. Just like Dr. Miota used to do. I felt more afraid this time. I could manipulate around Dr. Miota, but Manny was tough as nails.

I let my mind wander back again to the more comfortable places it knew—Jonathan and I running down the street together, eating sushi together years later, golfing on a near-deserted course. I was no longer in a roomful of addicts being pushed toward a "well" I dreaded to go near. I relived the memories with my family as the images melted together in my mind. I was in the comforting company of my loved ones. The rush from a narcotic or tranquilizer might have almost felt the same.

Manny saw me relax a little and jarred me back. "Scott, stick with the program. Now move to the edge of the well," he said firmly.

I felt trapped. I wanted to just open my eyes and run out of the room. I wanted to just run!

I started to cry. "I can't go there, Manny. It's too hard."

"Just keep going, you're doing great," he continued. "Now, what do you see?"

My tense body began to shake. In my mind I moved up to the edge of the well. I sobbed as I peered down into the dark well in my mind, into a bottomless abyss. *Oh, beauty I found in this Heaven and Earth, where from lonely darkness I have been led.*

I knew what was down there at the bottom. I knew what I had been running from! *Now I am bold and lay unafraid, with a lifetime of knowledge to comfort my head.*

"Come on, Scott, what do you see down there? Tell us where that pain's really been coming from." *Lift up my Spirit and I shall be free to follow Nature in her infinite path.*

"What is it that's been hurting you?" *To ramble the universe without passion or pain . . .*

"What is it about you and Jonathan that's been eating you alive?" Manny prompted again.

Then I heard Ryan's voice—the last person in that room I ever thought would speak. "Come on, bro', talk to us," he said softly, almost compassionately. *Oh Heavenly Host, bear me no wrath!*

Alone and vulnerable in the well, I suddenly heard Jonathan's name in my head and I broke down. I began crying harder, gasping for air. I could no longer bear to live with what I was suffering. The image of my father standing in the ICU waiting room materialized in my mind and I remained in that dark well. I had to break free of the painful memory. I sputtered out: "I think—god, I think I killed him! I think I killed my brother!

The Silent Demise

I awoke with the dawn and the spring's first breath
To watch as the earth bloomed from under the clouds.
In awe did I ponder on this glorious morn'
That shiver of death that hung like a shroud.

To watch did I of the tall trees that swayed
And whose shadows danced with the ascending sun,
Of the birds that soared on their endless flight
Where soon I shall fly—where wings I'll have none.

I gaze at this world through my limited eyes
Of life's golden moments now blemished with rust.
What beauty one finds with the calling of day,
But come night all dear life is returned to its dust.

For every new sun that soars above Earth,
And for each new tide that rushes the shore,
A baby is born to the hands of Time
And a life beholds springtime nevermore.

The fragrance of lilacs rides with a breeze,
The warmth of the day now touches the earth.
And I, so silent, glimpse the last of spring
As hence, I return to the home of my birth.

Shed not a tear, for though I'll be lost
The sun will shine and the wind will blow,
And those that are born with the ages to come
Shall walk in this Springtime and see what I know.

Oh beauty I found in this Heaven and Earth,
Where from lonely darkness I have been led.
Now I am bold and lay unafraid
With a lifetime of knowledge to comfort my head.

Lift up my Spirit and I shall be free
To follow Nature in her infinite path,
To ramble the universe without passion or pain,
Oh Heavenly Host, bear me no wrath!

—Jonathan Elliot Davis

17

A Life Beholds
Springtime Nevermore

SHERMAN OAKS MEDICAL CENTER
Intensive Care Unit Waiting Room
July 23, 1993
12:35 PM

I think we're losing Jonathan." My father's desperate words tore through me like a butcher's knife. I had been nurturing a tiny fragment of hope that Jonathan might pull through again this time, but it would not be so.

For a second I just stood there, frozen, not wanting to move and to play out the reality before us. Jonathan had been hospitalized several times since he had been diagnosed with AIDS. He had endured life-threatening pneumonias, severe abdominal infections, and exhausting anemia. Like the brave sailor he was, Jonathan had braved the bitter elements of his disease as he would a stormy ocean spraying in his face. Somehow, he had always found the calmer waters. Why, then, should this day be any different?

But this day *was* very different. I found Jonathan sitting straight up in bed, gasping and arching his head forward to draw every drop of air from his oxygen mask. His deeply sunken eyes reflected a fear I had never seen.

A chest x-ray hanging on a light box in his room revealed the reason for his distress. Both his lung fields were nearly white, full of fluid and inflammation. Only one small dark area remained in his right lung. That was the only healthy air pocket he had left. He could barely breathe.

His blood pressure had dropped to a critically low level, sounding a piercing alarm from the automatic blood pressure cuff. His nurse quickly came into the room and silenced the alarm. Another alarm from the EKG monitor over Jonathan's head then took its place, indicating that abnormal heartbeats were replacing his once-stable heart rhythm. The lack of oxygen and blood pressure were forcing his weakened heart to work even harder. Jonathan was struggling to survive.

In the midst of the chaos, someone in the room quietly pleaded, "Please, someone, do something. Do something." I don't even remember who it was.

I wanted to do something, but I also did not want to take my eyes off Jonathan for a moment. I feared it might be the last time I saw him alive. But I looked up upon hearing that. I was a doctor and someone wanted *something* done.

Jonathan's nurse had left the room but then returned within minutes. "We're trying to call Jonathan's doctor," she said anxiously, "but for some reason he's not responding yet. We're still trying."

I looked up and my mother locked on my gaze. Her expression seemed to beg me to do something, as though I were the only one in the room who could. Jonathan was in pain and near death. Someone needed to do *something!*

At that moment, I honestly could not think of what to do. I just wanted to see my brother free of the misery he was suffering. In the company of our loved ones, I suddenly felt so alone in the field.

I frantically said to the nurse, "Please, can you just turn up his morphine pump now? He needs to be more comfortable!"

For a moment, she looked at me hesitantly. I was not his doctor, but I was a doctor, and for the moment I was *it.*

"Please!" I repeated.

Reluctantly, she pressed a button on the morphine pump unit at the bedside. It whirred for several seconds, firing more narcotic into Jonathan's intravenous line. The entire process only took several seconds to empty the bolus of morphine into him. With Jonathan writhing uncomfortably, it seemed to take an hour.

"Can you give him more Valium, too?" I asked tearfully. "He—he needs it!" Without a pause this time, the nurse withdrew a syringe from her pocket and pushed the entire contents into my brother's IV line.

Several seconds later his taut, frail body began to relax. His head eased back onto the pillow. His rapid breathing began to slow to a more quiet and comfortable rate. The potent combination of narcotics and tranquilizer in his system seemed to ease the pain and the struggle. Perhaps, I thought, it might buy Jonathan some needed energy to safely sneak past this new crisis.

The nurse then did something that once again tore at the hope I was trying to rebuild. She walked over to the EKG monitor over Jonathan's head and turned it around so we could not see the screen. I had seen nurses do this many times in front of family members. I knew she had turned the screen away to hide the telltale "flatline" of death that would show on the monitor. With this small but caring act, she hoped to lessen the shock of Jonathan's inevitable final moment. Up to that moment, I still believed Jonathan might miraculously pull through—just once more. I knelt by Jonathan's side and took his hand. "It's okay, Jon, we're all here. Just go to sleep now," I whispered. "We'll see you soon."

I held his hand and, for a fraction of a second, felt one of his weak fingers press into my palm. The gentle squeeze was almost imperceptible, but it was the most powerful grip I had ever experienced. In the only way Jonathan could at that moment, he said, "I love you, and I'm leaving."

My brother took a deep breath—his last—and exhaled gently. Only two minutes after I had pleaded to his nurse for more morphine and Valium, he did something I always feared but did not expect at that moment. He died.

> *Shed not a tear for though I'll be lost*
> *The sun will shine and the wind will blow,*
> *And those that are born with the ages to come*
> *Shall walk in this Springtime and see what I know.*

With my head on the mattress next to Jonathan, I cried for what seemed like an hour. (Later I would find that only minutes had passed.) When I lifted my head up, I found myself alone in the room with him. Strangely, I had heard no one leave.

I stood up, suddenly feeling weak and exhausted, and I moved to the head of the bed. Jonathan appeared completely peaceful for the first time in ages. The muscles in his face had relaxed unevenly, giving the illusion he was smiling that half-crooked smile I knew so well.

I leaned over and kissed him on the forehead. "Good-bye, Jon," I whispered. Then, even more quietly, I whispered, "I love you."

I had never told him that before. I never felt I needed to. Now, a sharp pang of guilt ran through me that he would never hear those words from me. I wished desperately his eyes would open once more to hear me tell him I loved him. Jonathan, of course, did not respond.

As I stood back up to leave, I brushed against the morphine pump catheter still threaded into his arm.

"Can you just turn up his morphine pump?"

"Can you give him some more Valium, too?"

The orders I had given the nurse only minutes before suddenly flashed back to me. Jonathan was dying at that moment; we all knew that. I didn't want to think—I didn't want to believe—that somehow I had hastened his death. Actually, at that moment, I just didn't want to think at all. I took a deep breath and walked out. I would not think about it.

Two days later I would find a bottle of tranquilizers in Jonathan's bedroom drawer at home. With that, I found a way to never think about it again.

Oh Heavenly Host, bear me no wrath!

18

Memory Unforsaken

*T*he laughter in a darkened Hollywood theater was hysterical and infectious. It rippled like a wave throughout the packed rows of giggling theater patrons.

On the large screen, the comedian Groucho Marx, in his usual form, was paying a less-than-complimentary remark to his love interest, the portly Margaret Dumond.

"Do you know you look like the Prince of Wales?" he gently cooed to her.

"Really?" she blushed coyly.

"Oh yes! And when I say Wales, I mean whales!" The audience again howled with laughter.

The loud chortles and chuckles throughout the theater were indistinct compared to my own father's very distinctive laugh in the darkness. It had a fine, grating quality, like two bricks being rubbed together. His laugh was so unique that all of those seated around us would turn and stare to see just where such a noise was coming from. In between giggles, my father would happily repeat the punch line of the last onscreen comment, as to keep the amusement going for all of us. "When I say Wales, I . . . mean . . . *whales!*" Dad repeated, laughing between breaths, before the bricks rubbed together again for a few more seconds.

Sitting next to him in the dark theater were Neil, Jonathan, and me, busy laughing like mad hyenas ourselves. We were enjoying one another's company as much as Groucho and *his* brothers on-screen. We did not know at the moment that, sitting several rows behind us, was Groucho Marx himself! Then eighty years old, he had decided to take in one of his own movies from forty years before.

When we left the darkened theater after the show, our stomach muscles in knots from laughing, we noticed a commotion in the lobby. Our father recognized Groucho Marx and told us who he was. Groucho—adorned by a red beret and a young, tall, voluptuous blonde—was easy to recognize. Neil walked up to Groucho and said shyly, "I liked your movie very much, Mr. Marx."

Groucho looked down at Neil and patted his head. "You're a very nice boy," he said in a deep, throaty whisper. The years of cigar smoking had likely taken their toll on his voice.

Having just seen the larger-than-life Groucho on the big screen, Neil walked away as though in blissful shock, with the biggest smile I had ever seen on his face. One might have thought his head had just been patted by God's own hand.

Twenty years later, I tried to hold on to that distant happy memory as I sat in Manny's circle. I now felt completely drained of energy, having just revealed the details of my last moments with Jonathan. I no longer wanted to run away, but just to sit there and allow those happier, carefree family memories to wash over me again and cool the fire from the more recent painful past.

"How you feelin', man?" Ryan was the first to speak to me.

The fourteen pairs of eyes in the circle around me were staring at me, glistening. The looks now seemed much more caring and sympathetic than they had been earlier. I had finally revealed that truth at the core of my grief. The bare honesty had connected with my peers and seemed to bring them closer. Even Ryan was moved.

"How you feelin', man?" Two days before that meeting, all I was feeling was the crushing weight of a thousand sins on my shoulders. The intense Oregon rain was pelting the large, lush lawn in the middle of the Springbrook campus as I ran across it. I darted into a small building on the other side to escape and ran down a narrow staircase.

I was trying to get away from everyone and everything. I was hurting!

Ten minutes before this escape across the campus, counselor Manny informed me in his office I would not be at Springbrook for three or four weeks, as I thought. I would instead be required to stay for three full months of treatment. It seemed at the time like a life sentence.

It hit me hard! I would be separated from my wife and family for a long time, and our bank accounts would undoubtedly be drained to pay for my treatment. My selfish need to escape my pain would now separate me from those I loved and cared for. Another loss!

I ran down the stairs and into an empty bathroom. I locked the door behind me and went into one of the stalls to block any sound.

I then did something I had not done in a very long time.

I allowed myself to simply feel what I was feeling. I cried as I never cried before. I felt I was here in treatment in the company of strangers. I was all alone in the field again.

"How you feelin', man?" Now, two days later, I was surrounded in Manny's circle by a new family of loved ones—thirteen men who shared my disease of addiction. They knew what I'd done and where I'd been, yet they still wanted to help me get to where I needed to be.

All along, no matter how much I had tried to fool myself, I had needed to be where I was—seeking help. In that moment of honesty and truth, I had finally broken free.

"Welcome to a seat in recovery, Scott!" Manny chided. It had been sheer hell, but I had earned my seat.

19

A Lifetime of Knowledge

May 1999
Five Months after Springbrook

*F*ive months after I completed treatment at Springbrook, I sat alone downstairs in my mother's house in Northridge, California, where Jonathan and I had grown up. It was 9:00 AM and the house was still pin-drop quiet.

The chronic abdominal pain that had plagued me for years was now completely gone. Within days after finally breaking my tortured silence at Springbrook, the pain had miraculously disappeared.

All the physicians in the past had believed my pain had been caused by some physical problem that required complicated surgical correction. My pain was real, but the doctors had simply been looking in the wrong place. Had they been able to search my head and my heart, they would have discovered the intense pain of grief, loss, guilt, and shame that had been festering there like an abscess.

> *The word of God is living and active. Sharper than any double-edged sword, it cuts deep to separate soul from spirit; joint from bone. It judges the thoughts and purposes of the heart. Nothing God created is hidden from Him. His eyes see everything. He will hold us accountable for all that we do. (Hebrews 4:12–13 NIV).*

The treatment I received at Springbrook was far simpler than the medical specialists could have ever hoped for—simply talking openly with others who could understand, and from there learning how to move forward. The drugs had deepened my problems but had not been the problem; I was the problem I had tried to run away from.

Now I was finally free of the pain. Within weeks after graduating from the treatment center, the morphine pump was shut off permanently. One more surgical procedure several weeks later removed the pump altogether.

I now stared at the glass coffee table in front of me, deep in thought. Suddenly, as if taking a mental trip in a time machine, I imagined an evening twenty years before. The marred glass table in front of me was now unscratched, and on it sat several partially filled glasses of alcohol. Mom and Dad had served the predinner cocktails to some friends before they all left for an evening out, and they had left the glasses on the table.

Jon and I, then thirteen, and brother Neil ran around the table, drinking up what was left of the wonderfully forbidden brew. This was a ritual we happily repeated as often as the opportunity presented itself—usually every weekend. The combined excitement of being home alone and getting drunk was too much for us to pass up!

I watched the young Jonathan happily drink up his share and then run giddily through the downstairs rooms. He stopped and looked at me with his famous half-crooked smile, then darted upstairs into our shared bedroom. "Come on, Scott, follow me!" he laughed as he disappeared down the hall. He was gone, and so was the memory.

I sat, staring at where he had run so many years before. A bright morning ray of sun streaked into the bedroom from the upstairs skylight. I missed him terribly. At that moment, looking upstairs from the living room, I would have given anything to see Jonathan run back out of the bedroom.

I'm not sure what compelled me in my dark mood to walk upstairs and into the bedroom, but I did. As I entered the room, I remembered how it had looked just after Jonathan's death, when I had returned from the funeral. On the side of the room facing me, a large picture window had filled the room with bright, warm sunlight. The room had looked like a hospital room. The air was fresh and clean but still held heaviness, as though illness had been there. Dresser drawers on both sides of the room were partially opened, some filled with medical supplies: bandages, gauze pads, plastic bags full of saline, tubing for intravenous fluid feedings. One large drawer nearly overflowed with pill bottles. The descriptions on the bottle labels spoke of the extent of Jonathan's illness: antibiotics; powerful medicines to control vomiting, abdominal spasms, and diarrhea; painkillers and sedatives. I had picked up one nearly full bottle of sedatives, hesitated for a moment, and then put the bottle in my pocket. They certainly came in handy when my emotions started rising toward the surface again. *Damn if I'd let those emotions out!*

Now, four and a half years later, all remnants of that bedroom infirmary were gone. The heavy oak desk and dressers remained, but all of the medical supplies had been swept clean. The air was fresh and dust free this time, sweetly smelling of cinnamon deodorizer instead of antiseptic.

I walked across the bedroom, over to a small dresser next to the corner oak desk. This dresser was Jonathan's favorite, where he kept many of his prized possessions. I sat down and pulled open the bottom drawer. Magic tricks he'd kept from childhood, a dusty old family photo album, and ancient school report cards were scattered in the drawer.

I picked up the photo album and let it fall open. A picture revealed one of my favorite memories. Jonathan and I were standing together on the deck of a cruise ship, smiling and tanned, with nothing but the sparkling Caribbean Sea behind us. It had been taken one month before I read the doctor's letter announcing his HIV infection, when my world suddenly changed. In the photo we stood on the ship's deck, oblivious to the future and still like the young and innocent twins who ran happily down the neighborhood streets. In that moment, a carefree life was ours for the asking.

I pulled open the next drawer up. Several of Jonathan's brightly colored favorite sweaters were neatly folded. I was just about to close the drawer when I noticed the edge of a small wooden box in the back, underneath the sweaters. Jonathan had always been a private, secretive person, and a glimmer of excitement suddenly ran through me that I might find something revealing.

I pulled out the box. Oddly, this was the very same box where I had found the letter. What would I find in it this time? My hands trembled slightly as I once again opened Jonathan's "Pandora's box." Inside, I found many typewritten pages neatly stacked. I pulled the pages out and began to read. I could not believe what I had found.

They were poems that Jonathan had written. And there was not just one, but an entire collection written over the years. I picked up a page and began to read. I could hear Jonathan's voice speaking the words to me, sounding so much like my own. Focused on Jonathan's voice, I listened as he read his poetry to me. He began to read of his intense desire for love and to be loved:

> When Love calls, all that hear its magical tune listen,
> Awaiting the sound of the pure bells
> And the gentleness of the flute.
> . . . As dark as the midnight sky
> And as bright as the brilliancy of a noonday sun.

He read to me of his incredible fortitude and his will to survive:

> I, like the mountains that rise to such heights,
> Then crumble like sand to the wind-beaten dust,
> By a force which towers any deity of might,
> Through will I survive, then fall I must.

He read of his strong belief in God's awesome power and compassion:

I am the Guardian, the Keeper of Life,
The Tamer of the lion, the Demon in the lamb.
I am the Heaven and I am the Hell,
Yes, I am Eternal
I Am.

He even laughed to me about his own desperate fate:

"Then Good night," said Honor,
With one final breath.
"Farewell," whispered Life.
"Have some wine," smiled Death.

And Jonathan cried in agonizing silence about his fear of never leaving his isolated world:

Yes, there is a space to where I can go.
But though tragic and grateful and never still awed,
Does this silence so painful hinder my reach
To the light of Dear God, from this darkness so flawed.

I looked up from my reading. Jonathan's cat, Allston, had quietly wandered into the room and sat down barely a foot from me, but I hadn't noticed. He eyed me as if to say, "Hey, aren't you going to include me in what you're doing?"

Jonathan had been a quiet, darkly private man. He had never revealed his incredible gift of words to anyone until that moment. I had known him for thirty-three years and thought I knew him so well. Through his poetry, he spoke to me with words I had never heard him use, of emotions I had never seen him show. *Tragic and grateful, indeed.*

These were more than just words on pieces of paper; these were the unspoken expressions of a brother I really never knew, but thought I did. Perhaps it was our bond as twins that just made it seem like I knew all there was to know about him. I wished I had known this real Jonathan while he was still alive. To me, Jonathan's outside world had always seemed bleak and desperate in the face of his disease. I had felt swallowed up in the desperation I felt. Jonathan's poetry now painted a much different picture of my brother, in his own words. It reflected a heart that had been filled with such courage and strength. It revealed a fear of the unknown but also an acceptance of a loving and compassionate God who would guide him through his trials. Jonathan's poetry even illuminated his steadfast determination, that he chose to carry on despite the incredible odds.

Still stunned by what I had found, I stood up to leave. I held the poems tightly, as though they were some long-lost bridge I'd found to this new relationship. I turned to walk out of the bedroom. In the corner of my eye, I saw Allston still staring intently at something in the area that I had just left. Turning around, I noticed one of the poems had fallen out of the stack, unnoticed. *How did that happen?* I picked it up.

I thought I had read every poem carefully, every line word for word. But somehow I had missed this last one. As I read the poem, my hands began to tremble. When I finished reading, I slumped back to the floor and began to cry quietly.

This poem, unlike any of the others, seemed to reveal the one thing that mattered most to Jonathan in his turbulent lifetime. It lit a very dark place in his heart and soul that he had kept hidden. Something that Jonathan never revealed during his life comforted me greatly after his death. With tears in my eyes, I felt that I held the very bridge between us, and I read on:

Common Man

To the world I am a breathless heart,
A life eclipsed by a beckoning Hand.
Now my ears fail to hear and my lips fail to part,
But my soul still knows of a life so grand.

I speak not of possessions that someday I might hold.
Their true worthy value is little to own.
No, it is the love of my loved ones that I am compelled
To proclaim as the greatest possession I've known.

In the sweetest of days, they brought laughter and hope,
How these all seemed the very best days of my life.
In the most bitter of moments their love urged me to cope
With matters before me that now yield such strife.

It is they, my companions, who have shared in my world,
Who have given more than taken, with few reasons why.
It is for them I am grateful, and my soul here unfurled
To claim I am a common man who hurts to say good-bye.

This life so filled with promise was not without remorse,
Of dreams that I'd forsaken, of goals I'd not attained.

For life so wrought with challenge was still so wonderful a course,
Where footsteps I have planted will remain.

Hear my soul so gently speak, bitter not for what God has taken,
For triumph and misfortune knows every mortal man.
Let me always live within your hearts, my memory unforsaken,
And I shall always know just how fortunate I am.

—Jonathan Elliot Davis

It was family—*our family*—that had been a sanctuary for
Jonathan. It was from us that he had drawn his comfort. For
that "common man," his family was indeed his one place of
serenity, his one strong thread of sanity where he could find
refuge from his demons.

In my own mind, *after* his death, I had also tried to keep
those sweet family memories alive. As I fought my way past my
own demons, I had carried the same lamplight Jonathan held
until he died. Its bright beam had illuminated a path for us
both, back to safe and happy family times. I had thought about
it. Jonathan had written about it. We both found consolation
in it.

We were twins, remember?

20

Hope Can Surge Miles

*D*o you know what you found, man?" my Narcotics Anonymous sponsor, Hank, asked me. Hank nodded to one of Jonathan's poems I held in my hand. We were standing together just outside the doorway of a church meeting place. The Narcotics Anonymous meeting inside was just wrapping up. I was just about to leave when Hank's question encouraged me to stay for a few more moments to hear him out.

I had found Hank as a sponsor almost immediately after I started attending Narcotics Anonymous meetings. Hank had twenty-one years of sobriety. He always felt that he was "never wrapped too tight from day one." He kept coming to meetings himself and participating just to keep from "unwrapping" any further. Just talking with Hank for a few minutes always made me feel better. And I so desperately wanted to feel better.

The meetings were a mandatory part of my own recovery

program; the California Medical Board required me to attend them or risk losing my license. I knew how important the meetings were to my recovery just the same.

"Do you know what you found, man?"

I did know what I had found in Jonathan's poetry, or at least I thought I knew. But I still looked at Hank, puzzled. He was always good at seeing the other side of a situation, the truly revealing side I never thought of. Perhaps I had missed something here as well.

"Look," he continued, "the way I see it, Jonathan suffered with AIDS, and he died. You were just like him, suffering with his illness—but you lived. You're a survivor, man. Your brother died and gave you this incredible gift to survive with, to move forward with." Hank motioned to the poem in my hand. "I think he wants you to know him better now than you ever did when he was alive. I think what you found was his gift to you."

"His gift? Why couldn't he just give me his *gift* before he died?" I asked, challenging Hank. I had been so grateful to find Jonathan's poems, but lately I had been dealing with some bitterness, too.

"That was the Jonathan back then, the brother that didn't know how to let you in." Hank paused for a few seconds, letting the words sink in. "This is Jonathan now," he continued, "the one who wants you to know him. So stop this bullshit feeling sorry for yourself. Make something out of all of this. Live your life the way Jonathan could have lived it himself—if he had the chance."

I turned away from Hank, frustrated and confused. Live Jonathan's life? I had trouble living my own life, for me. How could I live it for him? Hank grabbed my shoulders and turned me around again. He seemed to know what I was thinking. "You can't live it *with* him anymore, Scott," he said, "so live it *for* him. You go home to that family of yours. You hold on to your mother, your father, your brother, your wife, your children, and all those wonderful, crazy family memories you talked about that kept you surviving. Jonathan showed you what he'd been holding on to." Hank again motioned to the poem I still had in my hand. "Maybe you never realized it, but you've been holding on to the other end all this time." He laughed.

I turned away and walked several steps toward the parking lot. I stopped for a minute, reflecting on what my sponsor had just said. Maybe Hank was right; perhaps the gift I had been given *in* life was the gift *of* life. I had been given a treasure to live my life the way Jonathan could have lived it—if he'd had the chance. With his courage and his passion, I only imagined what he could have enabled himself to become.

In my earlier, drug-addicted state, I could never have imagined this newfound courage and passion for living that was mine to grasp. Then, I had just wanted to survive. Now I realized I could do so much more with my life.

I turned around. Hank was still standing in the doorway. "Hey, Hank," I said. "So, what do you do when your dreams start to finally exceed your expectations?"

Hank looked toward the group of recovering addicts leaving the meeting room, and then smiled back at me. "If I were you," he whispered loudly, "I'd keep it to myself!"

I walked toward the parking lot. Hank called out to me, "Scott, you know you really didn't kill your brother, right?" I stopped in my tracks. Hank had hit a chord that resonated throughout my body. But he was right. I had not killed

Jonathan, and I had finally realized it that day at Springbrook in Manny's sharing circle when I had poured out my heart to the men there. On that day at Jonathan's bedside, I had implored the nurse to push more morphine and Valium. Jonathan was obviously in agonizing distress. My intense emotional pain at that moment may have been equal to his physical pain. An extra bolus of drugs at that moment felt comforting for both of us.

But I did not kill Jonathan. God took Jonathan at a moment I believe was destined, just as I was destined by God's miraculous power to be there at his bedside when he died, holding his hand. For years after Jonathan's death, I bore a feeling of guilt because I continued to live after he died. As I unloaded that pain in Manny's circle, I began to realize that, in reality, I had been blessed by being there. I was there for Jonathan at that final moment, as I always had been during his life. God had given me the gift of being the closest person to Jonathan since birth, up to the moment of his final living experience. It had taken me years to fill up a well of pain, and with this new self-discovery, only minutes to empty it in Manny's sharing circle.

After his death I would finally begin to understand him; I would understand the pain that must have ebbed and flowed beneath his surface as well as his passions for living. In God's divine way, I was not meant to know, not meant to understand until my own life could be tested. Jonathan had been like a miser with his golden words. I could now finally share the wealth.

Yes, I *had* played a part in Jonathan's death—I had stood by his side and loved him as he passed on.

In death, he was teaching me how to live.

21

How Fortunate I Am

I drove back home to the small two-bedroom apartment. I entered the dark bedroom. Rebecca was sleeping soundly. Quietly I undressed, slipped into bed, and closed my eyes. I was exhausted but excited, too.

Hank was right. I had spent far too much time "living Jonathan's life." It was time to start living my own again! I took a deep breath and slowly exhaled, feeling myself relax for a change.

Where do I go from here? I didn't know. But just for the day, just for the moment, it really did not matter. I had all that I could have asked for at that moment. I had my life. I had a family that loved me, which I loved in return. And I had Jonathan: I was no longer all alone in that field.

My exhaustion finally overcame my excitement, and I quickly drifted off to sleep—naturally, without sedatives, with a feeling of peace.

The dream started the same way it always did. Jonathan and I were eight years old again, laughing and running down the quiet neighborhood sidewalk. Our twin steps were in tandem, as always, as we raced between two houses into the backyard. The backyard changed into a large field dotted with grassy knolls and beautiful sunflowers. I raced ahead of Jonathan, still laughing and waving my arms, relishing the open space. I urged him to catch up to me, and then I turned around, afraid for a moment of what I might see.

There was Jonathan, catching up to me, but he was now thirty-three years old, as I was. His face and eyes were no longer sad and sunken, as I had feared they would be. Instead, they were full and bright with youth. His body was robust and seemed to radiate energy. His ever-present, half-crooked smile beamed with real happiness as he caught up to me, breathing heavily from the run.

"What's a guy got to do to keep up with you?" he laughed, in between breaths.

"Nothing," I said. "Not anymore."

I threw my arms around him and finally whispered something I had never said to him before while he was alive. "I love you, Jon."

"I love you, too, Scott."

Jonathan and I, "The Twins," held each other for a minute in the middle of the field. Then we turned and walked, side by side, farther into the open grassland. The dark alley between the houses grew smaller and smaller behind us as we moved in a totally different direction from where we had been.

As I lay there dreaming, I'm sure I was wearing a half-crooked smile.

Epilogue

On my office wall at the renowned Betty Ford Center, a large poster depicts a beautiful image of a forested mountain range at sunset. Its caption in large bold letters reads, "ATTITUDE. What happens *to* a man is less significant than what happens *within* him." What has happened within me and what I do with those emotions are now the keys to my recovery.

Today, I *am* a recovering addict. I am also a loving son, a caring husband, a faithful Christian,* a father smitten with the joy of parenthood, and a brother discovering a deeper connection with both Neil and Jonathan.

Today I now channel the lessons I have learned personally and professionally through my own addiction and recovery into my work. As of this writing, I have become the Addiction Medicine Physician for the Betty Ford Center, one of the most widely recognized and respected centers for the treatment of addictions. Each day I am rewarded when one more suffering,

---

*After I married Rebecca, I began accompanying her to her church services on Sundays. With each Sunday, I felt more spiritually connected with the pastor's messages, the encouragement to open my heart up to God and to Jesus Christ, and to love and to be loved unconditionally. I felt a stronger pull toward that connection than I had found in Judaism. I decided to become a Baptist.

addicted soul learns, as I did, to look beneath their skin and uncover their own healing truth. Freedom from the past and growing acceptance of the recovery process ahead often follows their inner revelation.

In the aftermath of the pain and chaos that once was, the budding hope for a happier, fuller life can blossom like a new spring rose.

Jonathan was right; hope *can* surge miles from the seas to the stars!

> *Hear my soul so gently speak,*
> *Bitter not for what God has taken,*
> *For triumph and misfortune knows every mortal man.*
> *Let me always live within your hearts, my memory unforsaken,*
> *And I shall always know just how fortunate I am.*

Afterword

*T*here is a myriad of words we use to describe the special part of us that governs how we live a meaningful life: the psyche, the soul, the self, the heart. No matter which term we use, this entity is our gyroscope, that uniquely human trait that centers us.

Here reside our core beliefs about who we are, what gives meaning to our lives, and how we fit into the world. Our hearts, minds, and souls show us how to lead what has been called an "authentic" life. Living authentically is not a guarantee of happiness; rather, it is a guarantee that we will experience life richly and genuinely, with moments of great courage.

This book is a cautionary tale, a story of what happens when we lose touch with our center . . . when, even though we believe we're doing our best to live a responsible and productive life, we ignore our wobbling gyroscope, deny our losses, and keep family secrets. In general, we try to measure up, meet family expectations, care for those in need, and silence the ache in our hearts.

The psyche, however, is a persistent and powerful messenger. When we ignore its distress calls, our hearts send them in another form. In this case, the message arrived in the form of debilitating physical pain. Yet the best of medical care could not begin to address this pain, because the cause wasn't physical. Prescription medications, while blunting the symptoms, couldn't cure the problem—because, frankly, the injury was to the psyche.

In cases like this, drugs do what they are supposed to: they allow us, for a time, to continue to ignore our emotional needs and to trudge along, doing all the "right things." Eventually, two things happen. First, the need for ever-larger doses of the drug grows as the pain grows. Addiction takes over, and the addict's life is consumed with the search for more drugs. Such craving moves us even farther away from the life we hoped for. Second, the drugs no longer work. They can't fill the hole in the soul, and we become so filled with pain and loneliness that we simply can't go on.

In the language of recovery, this moment in time is referred to as "hitting bottom"—when the soul can no longer tolerate what the body is doing. The caution light that has been flashing yellow for years has finally turned bright red. We can't quit and we can't continue. The message from the psyche has been received, loud and clear—an invitation, really—to change the way we have been living. At this point, we realize we're at a crossroads: we can choose to live the life our hearts yearn for, or we can return to the life of lonely desperation we've been living.

People wonder why addicts or alcoholics don't just quit. The answer is simply that it's too frightening. The prospect of spending an hour, much less a day, without access to the chemicals that have hooked them is terrifying. Equally terrifying is facing the demons we work so hard to deny. Facing fear, shame, guilt, and loss requires the utmost courage.

This special courage (or "fear that's said its prayers," to use a well-worn Alcoholics Anonymous [AA] phrase) comes about through the process of *en-couragement*. In the presence of courageous others, we find the courage to do what we couldn't do alone. We observe bravery, and somewhere deep in our hearts, we find the frightened, desperate motivation to try the same. Taking the risk to be just who we are meant to be, accepting our humanity, and finally living a life based on our understanding of our spiritual selves allows peace and serenity that can last the rest of our days.

When this cathartic moment arrives, the gyroscope will center itself and the soul will have been heard.

Nancy Waite O'Brien, Ph.D.
Betty Ford Center
Rancho Mirage, California

Appendices

Appendix 1: Glossary of Common Alcohol and Drug Addiction, Treatment, and Rehabilitation Terms

Abstinence: To refrain from the use of chemicals to which a person may have become addicted.

Addict: A person who has a craving for a mind-altering substance(s) that he/she cannot control.

Addiction: A dependence on alcohol, drugs, sex, and so on that becomes a physical and psychological craving with continued use despite adverse physical, mental, or social consequences.

Alcoholic: A person who develops an addiction to alcohol.

Alcoholics Anonymous (AA): A voluntary, anonymous, self-help organization of individuals who have a problem with consumption of chemicals, whether drugs or alcohol. Abstinence is achieved through a twelve-step process and a setting of one alcoholic sharing his/her similar experiences with another alcoholic.

Alcoholism: A chronic disease characterized by excessive consumption of and dependence on alcoholic beverages, leading to physical and psychological harm and impairing social and vocational functioning.

Al-Anon: A 12-step process for loved ones affected by an alcoholic/addict. It introduces alcoholism to those who may not understand the disease. Teaches coping skills and ways of providing support for the alcoholic/addict without enabling the addictive disease.

Amphetamines: Synthetic amines (uppers) that act on the central nervous system with a pronounced stimulant effect.

Barbiturates: A class of drugs used in medicine as hypnotic agents to promote sleep or sedation, or in the control of epilepsy. All are central nervous system depressants and are subject to abuse.

Binge drinking: The consumption of five or more alcoholic drinks in a row on at least one occasion.

Blood alcohol concentration (BAC): The amount of alcohol detected in the bloodstream, measured in percentages.

Chemical dependency: A syndrome characterized by a maladaptive pattern of substance use, leading to significant physical, psychological, or social distress (see Appendix 4A: Diagnostic Criteria for Chemical Dependence).

Cocaine: An alkaloid, methylbenzoylecgonine, extracted from the leaves of the coca tree. It is a central nervous system stimulant producing euphoric excitement.

Depressants: Drugs that reduce the activity of the central nervous system (alcohol, benzodiazepines, barbiturates, sedative-hypnotics, and narcotics are in this class).

Designer drugs: Illegal drugs are defined in terms of their chemical formulas. Designer drugs are all illegal drugs modified chemically to circumvent legal restrictions, usually drugs related to amphetamines. All can cause neurochemical brain damage.

Detoxification: A treatment to rid the body from addictive substances, such as drugs and/or alcohol.

Downers: Barbiturates, benzodiazepines, tranquilizers, and related drug depressants.

Drug: Any chemical substance that alters mood, perception, or consciousness.

Drug abuse: Pathological use of a prescribed or nonprescribed chemical substance (see Appendix 4B: Diagnostic Criteria for Substance Abuse).

Dual diagnosis: Substance abuse or dependency in addition to or coexisting with a psychiatric disorder.

Enabling: Allowing irresponsible and destructive behavior patterns to continue by taking responsibility for others and/or not allowing them to face consequences of their own actions.

Families Anonymous: A twelve-step, self-help recovery and fellowship of support groups for relatives and friends of those with alcohol, drug, or behavioral problems. They share similar experiences, strengths, and hope with one another and with new members.

Habituation: The result of repeated consumption of a drug that produces psychological but not physical dependence. The psychological dependence produces a desire (not a compulsion) to continue taking the drug for a sense of improved well-being.

Hallucinogen: Drugs that stimulate the central nervous system and produce varied changes in perception and mood.

Hashish: The concentrated resin of the marijuana plant.

Heroin: A semisynthetic derivative of morphine, used illicitly by injecting, smoking, or sniffing ("huffing"), which causes euphoria.

Inhalants: A variety of psychoactive substances inhaled as gases or volatile liquids. These include glue, gasoline, paint thinner, and other household products not considered to be drugs.

LSD: In the class of hallucinogens. When ingested, distorts perception of time and space, resulting in illusions and hallucinations.

Marijuana: The crushed and dried flowering top of the marijuana plant, abused by ingestion and smoking. The user acutely experiences a distorted sense of time and distance, impaired judgment, slowed reaction time, reduced attention span, and memory loss.

Methadone: A synthetic opiate with action similar to that of morphine and heroin, used legally for pain control and as a substitute for heroin in the treatment of heroin addiction.

Methamphetamine: A stimulant found in powder, pill, and capsule form that can be inhaled, swallowed, or injected. Physical effects of intoxication include alertness, euphoria, loss of appetite, dilated pupils, elevated heart rate, increased breathing, and elevated body temperature (also known as meth, crank, crystal, ice, glass, or speed).

Narcotics: A class of depressant drugs derived from opium or related chemically to compounds of opium that are highly addictive with regular use.

Narcotics Anonymous (NA): A self-help organization of

individuals who have a dependence on drugs and who are committed to abstinence.

Opiates: Drugs derived from opium, such as morphine and codeine, and the semisynthetic derivatives such as heroin.

PCP: A synthetic substance chemically related to ketamine. Signs and symptoms of use include blurred vision, diminished sensation, muteness, confusion, anxious amnesia, distortion of body image, thought disorders, and motor depression or stimulation, which may result in aggressive or bizarre behavior.

Physical dependence: The state whereby a person cannot function normally without the repeated use—and usually increasing frequency and amounts—of the drug. Discontinuation of the drug results in physical and psychic disturbances (see Appendix 4A: Diagnostic Criteria for Chemical Dependence).

Recovery: A lifelong process of change by an individual to abstain from alcohol or drug use.

Relapse: To fall back into the former state of drinking alcohol or using drugs once treatment or recovery has begun; the act of going back to old addictive behaviors or regressing from sobriety.

Sober living: A semistructured residential setting of alcoholics/ addicts who have completed treatment and need continued support in this setting, usually for up to one year.

Sobriety: Abstinence from consumption of alcohol or drugs.

Steroids: A large family of pharmaceutical drugs related to the adrenal hormone cortisone.

Stimulants: Drugs that increase the activity of the nervous system, causing wakefulness (also known as "uppers").

Tolerance: A state in which the body's tissue cells adjust to the presence of a drug. With tolerance, the body becomes accustomed to the presence of a drug in given amounts and eventually fails to respond to ordinarily effective dosages. Larger doses are then necessary to produce desired effects.

Twelve-step program: A process of abstinence, based on the twelve steps of Alcoholics Anonymous, now used by millions of alcoholics/addicts to develop and maintain abstinence from alcohol or drugs. The steps represent admitting to one's self that he/she has a problem with alcohol or drugs; a cleansing process of shame, guilt, and resentment; a character-building process; an amending process; and a process of giving back to others seeking recovery for the new life that one has received.

Withdrawal: Physical signs and symptoms manifested during detoxification from alcohol or drugs. Withdrawal effects vary, depending on the drug used and amounts, but commonly may include nausea, vomiting, insomnia, anxiety, convulsions, sweating, trembling, weakness, and seizures.

Appendix 2: Compendium of Alcohol and Drug Treatment Programs and Centers

I. BY TREATMENT ISSUE:

(For detailed information on each program, see state listing)

Adolescent Treatment:

Alldredge Academy: Davis, WV

Amity: Tucson, AZ

Aspen Achievement Academy: Loa, UT

The Camp Recovery Center: Scotts Valley, CA

Caron Foundation: Wernersville, PA

Cottonwood de Tucson: Tucson, AZ (Female only, chemical dependency, dual diagnosis, eating disorders)

Cumberland Heights: Nashville, TN

The Gables: Rochester, MN (Eating disorders, dual diagnosis)

Gray Wolf Ranch: Port Townsend, WA (Male only, thirty days through primary chemical dependency treatment required.)

Hazelden Center for Youth and Family: Plymouth, MN

Hazelden Chicago: Lombard and Deerfield, IL (Outpatient)

The Journey Home Recovery Center, Inc: Gonzales, LA (Low-cost, dual diagnosis)

Las Encinas Hospital: Pasadena, CA (Outpatient)

Matrix Institute: Los Angeles, CA (Dual diagnosis)

The Menninger Clinic: Houston, TX

Mirasol: Tucson, AZ (Female only, eating disorders)

Nexus Recovery Center, Inc: Dallas, TX (Female only)

Ohlhoff Recovery Programs: San Francisco, CA (Outpatient)

Pine Grove Next Step: Hattiesburg, MS

Provo Canyon School: Provo, UT (Secured facility)

Remuda Residential Ranch: Wickenburg, AZ (Female only, eating disorders)

River Oaks Psychiatric: New Orleans, LA
   (Dual diagnosis, trauma, eating disorders)

Rosecrance on Alpine: Rockford, IL

St. Christopher's: Galveston, TX (For young men ages 17 and older)

Sundown M Ranch: Yakima, WA

Touchstones: Orange, CA
   (Sliding scale, lower cost for Orange County residents)

Twin Town Treatment Center: Los Angeles, CA (Bilingual)

UCLA Neuropsychiatric Hospital: Los Angeles, CA (Dual diagnosis)

Village Counseling Breaking Free Program: Palm Desert/Desert Hot
   Springs/Coachella, CA

Visions Adolescent Treatment Center: Malibu, CA

Wilderness Treatment Program: Marion, MT

Detox:

Fountain Ridge: Las Vegas, NV

Hemet Valley Recovery Center: Hemet, CA

Loma Linda Behavioral Medicine Center: Redlands, CA

Dual Diagnosis:

Advanced Recovery Center: Delray Beach, FL (Gender relevant)

Alternatives: Los Angeles, CA (Gay, lesbian, bisexual, transgender)

Cirque Lodge: Sundance, UT (chemical dependency must be primary)

Cornerstone: Tustin, CA

Cottonwood de Tucson: Tucson, AZ

The Gables: Rochester, MN (Eating disorders, dual diagnosis)

Haight-Ashbury Free Clinics, Inc.: San Francisco, CA

Las Encinas Hospital: Pasadena, CA

Mayo Clinic: Rochester, MN

The Meadows: Wickenburg, AZ

The Menninger Clinic: Houston, TX

National Alcohol & Drug Treatment Program: Los Angeles, CA
    (Day care, low-cost, MediCal)

Pine Grove Next Step: Hattiesburg, MS

River Community: Azusa, CA (Financial assistance available)

River Oaks Psychiatric: New Orleans, LA

Sierra Tucson: Tucson, AZ

Transitions Recovery Program: North Miami Beach, FL

UCLA Neuropsychiatric Hospital: Los Angeles, CA

Wellness Resource Center: Boca Raton, FL

Eating Disorders:

Advanced Recovery Center: Delray Beach, FL (Gender relevant)

Alternatives: Los Angeles, CA (Gay, lesbian, bisexual, transgender)

Caron Foundation: Wernersville, PA

The Gables: Rochester, MN

The Meadows: Wickenburg, AZ

Mirasol: Tucson, AZ (Female only)

Monte Nido: Malibu, CA

Montecatini: Rancho La Costa, CA

Ohlhoff Recovery Programs: San Francisco, CA

Pavillon International: Mill Spring, NC

Progress Valley: Phoenix, AZ

Rader Institute: Oxnard, CA

Remuda Residential Ranch: Wickenburg, AZ (Female only)

River Oaks Psychiatric: New Orleans, LA

Rosewood Women's Center: Wickenburg, AZ
(Medically compromised patients accepted)

Sierra Tucson: Tucson, AZ

Sober Living by the Sea: Newport Beach, CA (Female only)

Transitions Recovery Program: North Miami Beach, FL

Turning Point of Tampa, Inc: Tampa, FL

Vista Taos: Taos, NM

Gambling:

The Meadows: Wickenburg, AZ

Pavillon International: Mill Spring, NC

Progress Valley: Phoenix, AZ

Gay/Lesbian:

Alternatives: Los Angeles, CA (Gay, lesbian, bisexual, transgender)

Pride Institute: MN/FL/IL/TX/NY

Gender Specific—Female:

Clare Foundation: Santa Monica, CA

Hacienda for Women: Desert Hot Springs, CA

Hazelden Women and Children's Recovery Community: New Brighton, MN

New Directions for Women: Costa Mesa, CA

Nexus Recovery Center, Inc.: Dallas, TX

Remuda Residential Ranch: Wickenburg, AZ (Female only, eating disorders)

Soroptomist International House of Hope: Banning/Desert Hot Springs/
Palm Springs, CA

Women in Recovery: Venice, CA

Gender Specific—Male:

Bishop Gooden Home: Pasadena, CA

Clare Foundation: Santa Monica, CA

Gray Wolf Ranch: Port Townsend, WA (Adolescent male, thirty days through
    primary chemical dependency treatment required)

The Ranch: Desert Hot Springs, CA

Sober Living by the Sea: Sunrise Recovery Ranch, CA

Hospitalization Programs:

Hemet Valley Recovery Center: Hemet, CA

Mayo Clinic: Rochester, MN

The Menninger Clinic: Houston, TX

Rosecrance on Harrison: Rockford, IL (Partial hospitalization)

Low-cost:

ABC Club: Indio, CA

Alternatives: Los Angeles, CA (Gay, lesbian, bisexual, transgender)

Amity: Tucson, AZ

Bishop Gooden Home: Pasadena, CA (Men only)

Camp Recovery Center: Scotts Valley, CA

Clare Foundation: Santa Monica, CA

CRI-HELP: North Hollywood, CA

Hacienda for Women: Desert Hot Springs, CA

Haight-Ashbury Free Clinics, Inc.: San Francisco, CA

Mile High Council on Alcohol and Drug Abuse: Denver, CO

National Alcohol & Drug Treatment Program: Los Angeles, CA
    (Day care, low-cost, MediCal)

New Found Life, Inc.: Long Beach, CA

Ohlhoff Recovery Programs: San Francisco, CA

Progress Valley: Phoenix, AZ

The Ranch: Desert Hot Springs, CA

Soroptimist International House of Hope: Banning/Desert Hot Springs/
    Palm Springs, CA

Village Counseling Breaking Free Program: Palm Desert/Desert Hot
    Springs/Coachella, CA

Nicotine:

Caron Foundation: Wernersville, PA

Hazelden—Your Next Step Tobacco Cessation Program: Center City, MN

Hilton Head Health Institute: Hilton Head, SC

Serenity Lane Health Services: Eugene, OR

Sundown M Ranch: Yakima, WA

Transitions Recovery Program: North Miami Beach, FL

Valley Hope: AZ/CO/KS/MO/NB/OK/TX

Pain Management:

Hemet Valley Recovery Center: Hemet, CA

Loma Linda University Behavioral Medicine Center: Redlands, CA

Proposition 36 Facilities:

ABC Club: Indio, CA

Cornerstone: Tustin, CA

Hacienda for Women: Desert Hot Springs, CA

The Ranch: Desert Hot Springs, CA

Village Counseling Breaking Free Program: Palm Desert/Desert Hot
    Springs/Coachella, CA

Relapse/Reluctant to Recover:

ABC Club: Indio, CA

Alina Lodge: Blairstown, NJ

Bishop Gooden Home: Pasadena, CA (Male only)

Cirque Lodge: Sundance, UT

Father Martin's Ashley House: Havre de Grace, MD

Hacienda for Women: Desert Hot Springs, CA

The Ranch: Desert Hot Springs, CA

Religious Philosophies:

Jewish: Gateways Beit T'Shuvah: Los Angeles, CA

Nondenominational Christian: Remuda Residential Ranch: Wickenburg, AZ
(Female only)

Seventh-Day Adventist: Loma Linda University Behavioral Medicine Center:
Redlands, CA

Seniors:

Hanley-Hazelden: West Palm Beach, FL

Hemet Valley Recovery Center: Hemet, CA

The Menninger Clinic: Houston, TX

National Alcohol & Drug Treatment Program: Los Angeles, CA (Day care,
low-cost, MediCal)

Sundown M Ranch: Yakima, WA

UCLA Neuropsychiatric Hospital: Los Angeles, CA

Sexual Compulsivity:

Alternatives: Los Angeles, CA (Gay, lesbian, bisexual, transgender)

The Meadows: Wickenburg, AZ

Pavillon International: Mill Spring, NC

Sober Living:

Alternatives: Los Angeles, CA (Gay, lesbian, bisexual, transgender)

Clare Foundation: Santa Monica, CA

Cornerstone: Tustin, CA

CRI-HELP: North Hollywood, CA

Hazelden Women and Children's Recovery Community: New Brighton, MN

Herbert House: Los Angeles, CA

Hope's Horizon: Palm Springs, CA

Gray Wolf Ranch: Port Townsend, WA (Adult/Adolescent. Male, thirty days
     through primary chemical dependency treatment required)

Sober Living by the Sea: Newport Beach, CA

Trauma:

The Life Healing Center of Santa Fe: Santa Fe, NM

Pavillon International: Mill Spring, NC

River Oaks Psychiatric: New Orleans, LA

Sierra Tucson: Tucson, AZ

Vista Taos: Taos, NM

Women with Children:

Hazelden Women and Children's Recovery Community: New Brighton, MN

New Directions for Women: Costa Mesa, CA

Nexus Recovery Center, Inc: Dallas, TX

Rosecrance on Harrison: Rockford, IL

Works with Court System:

Clare Foundation: Santa Monica, CA

Cornerstone: Tustin, CA

BETTY FORD CENTER SPECIFIC PROGRAMS

The Betty Ford Center is a nonprofit organization that provides treatment for the disease of alcoholism and other drug addiction for the entire family, including patients, their families, and their children. Our clinical staff provides a comprehensive continuum of care. We provide specialized treatment for licensed professionals.

Program	Length of Stay	Program Cost
Children's Program	4 days (Thurs–Sun) (ages 7–12)	No child turned away for lack of funds. Scholarships available.
Family Program (13 and older)	5 days (Mon–Fri)	$600
Outpatient[1] (18 and over)	8 weeks	$4,400[2]
Inpatient[1]/**Residential**[1] (18 and over)	30 days[3] 90 days	$21,000[4] $33,000[4]
Clinical Diagnostic Evaluation	3-day outpatient evaluation & recommendation	$3,300
Licensed Professionals[1] (with no licensing issues)	30 days[3]	$21,000[4]
Licensed Professionals[1]	90 days	$33,000[4]
Training	Various professional education programs	

[1] Includes one family member attending the family program at no additional cost.

(Cont'd on page 150.)

(Cont'd from page 149.)

[2] $500 of the required deposit is nonrefundable. Pricing is all-inclusive. Direct billing for contracted insurance companies.

[3] Extended care is available.

[4] Medically supervised detoxification is included; patient may remain in stabilization hall during this period. $5,000 of the required deposit is nonrefundable. Actual charges will vary depending on length of stay. Pricing is all-inclusive with the exception of medications and/or special services. Direct billing for contracted insurance companies.

Upon admission to the Betty Ford Center, patients begin detoxification and are evaluated by an interdisciplinary assessment team. An individualized treatment plan is created, and patients begin participating in their treatment as soon as possible. Actual length of stay may vary depending on individual patient needs.

CONTINUING CARE

Long-term recovery from addiction depends on the patient's daily involvement in maintaining a healthy personal program when he or she returns home, which includes participation in 12-step programs. To assist patients in making the transition home, each patient works with a continuing care counselor to design a structured plan of care that supports ongoing recovery. Alumni of the Betty Ford Center from the patient's home area offer support and encouragement to patients as they begin to participate in 12-step activities at home. Each patient is assigned an alumni contact who helps acclimate the newcomer to the local 12-step resources that support recovery. The Betty Ford Center also provides regularly scheduled telephone contact that lasts throughout the patient's first year following discharge. The telephone counselor offers encouragement and helps patients address relapse issues during early recovery, often the riskiest time for the newly recovering alcoholic or addict.

Betty Ford Center Outpatient/Family Services

Day Family Program

Five-day program (Monday–Friday)

Mon. 8:00 AM–3:00 PM

Tues./Wed. 9:00 AM–4:00 PM

Thurs. 8:30 AM–3:00 PM

Fri. 9:00 AM–3:00 PM

Offered every week, open to the public (including people with
  no patients at the Betty Ford Center)

Ages: 13 yrs. and up

Family Week is generally scheduled on the inpatient's third week (if the admission day is on Monday or Tuesday, count that as the first week) or generally fourth or fifth week of RDT (residential day treatment) patients' stay. The family counselor, along with the patient's counselor, make a determination about which week family interactions can be arranged in the patient's best interest. One person is covered under the patient's bill. General public family members with no patient in treatment at the Betty Ford Center are also welcome to register. Financial assistance available.

Holiday Inn Express: 760-340-4303

Phone menu: "Betty Ford Center Family Program"

Sitters come to Holiday Inn Express: Fri. and Sat.

Aunt Fran's shuttle service provided daily: 760-346-0828

Mother's Babysitting: 760-321-9294 , ext. 4114

Intensive Outpatient Treatment Program

Treats both substance abuse and codependency.

Eight-week program: Mon.–Fri., 5:30 PM–9:00 PM

Ages: 18 yrs. and up

Evening and Day Family Program available to patient's family members

Preferred admission days are Monday and Tuesday.

(Friday is not a billable day.)

Contact Admissions, ext. 4802

Evening Outpatient Family Program

Four nights: Mon.–Thurs. 5:45 PM–9:00 PM*

Offered one week per month for general public and families of outpatients.

Ages: 13 yrs. and up

Note: This program is not covered under "Patient's Bill."

*First night arrive at 5:00 PM

Children's Program

(not an outpatient program but listed here for your information)

Four-day program: Thurs.–Sunday 9:00 AM–3:00 PM
    (Thurs. check-in at 8:00 AM)

Offered three to four times per month on-site at the Betty Ford Center
    and at various off-site locations.

Groups are also regularly scheduled in the Dallas–Fort Worth
    Metroplex and in Denver.

Ages: 7–12
    Children from alcoholic and/or other drug-addicted families.

Parent(s), caregiver must participate first day for an hour and all day
Saturday and Sunday.

Contact Karen, ext. 4291

Scholarships available for those who qualify.

Adolescent Group

Ages: 13–18 years

Male/Female–English only

Tuesday nights from 4:30 PM–6:00 PM

Thirteen-week commitment

Contact Gisela Ghaemi, ext. 8013

Recovery Enrichment—Relapse Prevention Program

Ann and Tom Martin, Facilitators

(Not an outpatient program, but listed here for your information)

Five-day program (administered via Martins Counseling: 760-568-9233)

Prerequisite: ninety days sobriety prior to program and complete interview
with Martins Counseling.

Maximum participants: twenty

Contact Martins for basic information and registration

II. By State:

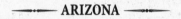

ARIZONA

Amity

520-749-2115

P.O. Box 32200

Tucson, AZ 85751

www.amityfoundation.com

Private nonprofit organization providing residential, transition, and continuance services. Amity provides living quarters as well as the daily therapeutic community model in which participants learn to live as a community, as well as receiving therapeutic individual services, family reunification services, and educational and vocational training. The holistic curriculum addressing family dynamics, prejudices, violations, individual strengths, trauma, and the development of emotional literacy help people expand both mind and spirit as part of daily community life. A minimum of six months is required. Locations in Arizona, California, and New Mexico.

Cottonwood de Tucson

Within Arizona: 520-684-3926

Outside Arizona: 800-632-3697

4110 West Sweetwater Drive

Tucson, AZ 85745

www.cottonwooddetucson.com

Four- to six-week adult treatment of co-occurring mental health disorders, such as depression, bipolar disorder, posttraumatic stress disorder, gambling, relationship, and sexual issues. The young adult program for ages 18–23 is intensive, goal-oriented, and includes a solid base of medical management, focus groups, Cottonwood Challenge Course, martial arts, rock and rope climbing, and individualized small specialty groups.

The adolescent girls' program is a dual diagnosis program working with chemical dependency with a strong emphasis on mental health issues. Each patient has a complete physical and psychiatric assessment. The forty-five-day intensive program includes a solid base of medical management, 12-step concepts, family involvement, group therapy, nutritional counseling, and individualized small specialty groups.

The Meadows

Within the United States: 800-632-3697

Outside the United States: 928-684-3926

1655 Tegner Street

Wickenburg, AZ 85390

www.themeadows.org

The Meadows is licensed as a Level I Psychiatric Acute Hospital by the Arizona Department of Health through the Department of Behavioral Health Services. They are licensed to provide psychiatric, detoxification, substance abuse, and partial hospitalization services. The 12-step–based program specializes in the treatment of trauma and addiction, including compulsive behaviors such as eating, gambling, work, love addiction-avoidance, co-dependency, and sexual disorders; psychological conditions, including post-traumatic stress disorder, obsessive-compulsive disorder, and dependent personality lifestyles; and affective disorders such as major depression, panic attacks, and bipolar disorder. Will work with insurance carriers and patients to review program costs and payment options.

Mirasol

888-520-1700

520-615-9323

7650 E. Broadway, Suite 303

Tucson, AZ 85710-3773

www.mirasol.net

Provides a unique, integrative treatment program providing recovery from eating disorders and healing chronic illnesses. Treatment consists of traditional therapies, individual psychotherapy, narrative therapy, trauma work, nutrition intervention, and a specialized tract on sexuality and eating disorders. The new adolescent eating disorder and obesity residential program for girls ages 12–17 is a sixty-day residential program treating anorexia, bulimia, binge eating, and obesity. Mirasol uses a variety of traditional therapies, individual psychotherapy, trauma work, nutritional intervention, and a specialized experiential tract utilizing martial arts, rocks and ropes, challenge courses, and animal therapy.

Progress Valley (Sober Living Residence)

480-315-1999

10505 N. 69th Street, Suite 1100

Scottsdale, AZ 85253

www.progressvalley.org

Progress Valley provides residential aftercare for those who are in the early stages of recovery from chemical dependency, as well as aftercare programs through comprehensive clinical and supportive services to adults with substance abuse and related disabilities such as an eating or gambling disorder. The foundation of the program is the belief that people seeking or maintaining recovery must be responsible for their financial, social, physical, and emotional behavior. The staff consists of both on-site professionals and outside consultants. Expectations for residents include a very full schedule of activities in addition to full-time employment.

Remuda Residential Ranch

800-445-1900

928-684-3913

One East Apache Street

Wickenburg, AZ 85390

www.remuda-ranch.com

Remuda Ranch is a biblically based program in a ranch setting offering intensive inpatient programs for women and girls suffering from anorexia, bulimia, and related issues.

Rosewood Women's Center for Anorexia, Bulimia, & Related Disorders

800-845-2211

928-684-9594

36075 South Rincon Road

Wickenburg, AZ 85390

www.rosewoodranch.com

Rosewood is a fourteen-bed inpatient treatment program designed to treat adult women 18 and older who are suffering from anorexia, bulimia, compulsive overeating, and related disorders. Treatment is based on a variable length of stay depending on medical acuity level and the individual needs of each patient. The average length of stay is forty-five days. Inpatient treatment at Rosewood includes a solid foundation in medical, psychiatric, clinical, and nutritional management. Components of the program include weekly individual sessions with the psychiatrist, primary care provider, and nutritionist. Daily activities include didactic sessions, twice-daily group psychotherapy, and special groups to address trauma, affective and cognitive development, body image development, and self-regulation strategies for relapse prevention. The multidisciplinary team consists of a psychiatrist, a registered nurse, Ph.D. and master's degree–level therapists, certified addiction counselors, and a nutritionist.

Sierra Tucson Intake

800-842-4487

39580 South Lago del Oro Parkway

Tucson, AZ 85739

www.sierratucson.com

Sierra Tucson is a dually licensed, accredited special psychiatric hospital and behavioral health center. Psychodrama, Eye Movement Desensitization and Reprocessing (EMDR), Somatic Experiencing, acupuncture, chiropractic services, and yoga, as well as more traditional group and cognitive-behavioral therapies are utilized. Sierra Tucson provides treatment for the following issues: chemical dependency, gambling, sexual addiction, dual diagnosis, trauma, eating disorders, and mood disorders.

Valley Hope Information

800-654-0486

Admissions: 800-544-5101

Inpatient Program (IP) in Chandler, AZ

Intensive Outpatient Program (IOP) in Phoenix and Tempe, AZ

www.valleyhope.com

Valley Hope is a nationally recognized, nonprofit organization dedicated to providing quality alcohol and drug addiction treatment services at an affordable price. Their individualized treatment plans are based on the 12-step philosophy with a strong emphasis on family participation, spirituality (nondenominational), and continuing care. Valley Hope operates IP and IOP treatment facilities in seven states—Arizona, Colorado, Kansas, Missouri, Nebraska, Oklahoma, and Texas.

—·— CALIFORNIA —·—

ABC Club

760-342-6616

44374 Palm Avenue

Indio, CA 92201

Low-cost treatment, $1,950 per month. Suggested treatment: ninety days up to one year. Sober living up to one year available. Also offers aftercare and family group.

Alternatives

800-342-5429

323-671-1600

2526 Hyperion Avenue, #4

Los Angeles, CA 90027

Ask for Bryan Fletcher or Michael Dutton when doing a direct transfer.

www.alternativesinc.com

Alternatives is the nation's only gay-owned and operated alcohol, drug, and mental health program whose leadership has provided more than thirty years of pride and service to the gay, lesbian, bisexual, and transgender community. Alternatives specializes in treating HIV/AIDS-related grief and loss. Our HIV specialists are available to address all medical concerns. Medicare and most insurance accepted. JCAHO accredited. Full residential program (therapy provided five days a week, six hours a day): $6,000/month; recovery plus (residential program, therapy provided three days per week, three hours a day): $3,200/month; sober living: $500/month. Accepts Medicare, private insurance on a case-by-case basis.

Bishop Gooden Home
626-356-0078
191 North El Molino Avenue
Pasadena, CA 91101
www.bishopgoodenhome.org

Bishop Gooden is a 12-step–based, all male, Commission on Accreditation of Rehabilitation Facilities (CARF) accredited treatment facility. The minimum length of stay is thirty days; the average length of stay is seventy-five days. Cost for treatment is as follows: thirty-day residential treatment: $3,750; day treatment plus (sober living provided): $2,750; IOP plus (sober living provided): $1,350. Bishop Gooden Home maintains contracts with some managed care providers such as Blue Cross of California, MHN (mental health network), Value Options, PacifiCare, and Kaiser Permanente.

The Camp Recovery Centers
877-577-6237
800-924-2879
3192 Glen Canyon Road
Scotts Valley, CA 95066
www.camprecovery.com

Located in the Santa Cruz Mountains in the San Francisco Bay Area. Lower-cost treatment for adolescents and adults. Detox, residential, day treatment, intensive outpatient, continuing care, and family program offered. Cost per day: Detox (adults and adolescents): $625/day for seven days; residential adult: $500/day; residential adolescent: $575/day. The length of stay is approximately thirty days. The Camp Recovery Centers work with most managed care health insurance organizations (HMOs), Union Trust Funds, Employee Assistance Programs, and accepts private funds as payment for treatment services at all levels of care.

Clare Foundation

310-314-6200

911 Pico Boulevard

Santa Monica, CA 90404

www.clarefoundation.org

Residential, outpatient, and community-based programs offer culturally sensitive English, Spanish, and American Sign Language recovery services to a diverse population of men, women, women with children, the deaf and hard-of-hearing, the homeless, and those facing criminal prosecution for drug and alcohol offenses. Programs include nonmedical detox, primary recovery support, long-term residential treatment, and sober living apartments, as well as transitional outpatient case management and community-based family services. The Clare Foundation no longer accepts phone assessments. They will only do face-to-face assessments on a first-come, first-served basis.

Cornerstone

800-385-9889

714-730-5399

13682 Yorba Street

Tustin, CA 92780

www.cornerstone-socal.com

Offers medically monitored detox, inpatient, outpatient, extended care, sober living homes, and an alternative sentencing program. Cornerstone is state licensed, certified, and probation approved. Offers treatment specific to dual diagnosis. Chemical dependency must be primary. Standard length of stay is two to four weeks with step down to residential, partial day treatment, or intensive outpatient based on insurance coverage. Is contracted with most major private healthcare providers.

CRI-HELP, Inc.

818-985-8323

11027 Burbank Boulevard

North Hollywood, CA 91601

www.cri-help.org

Low-cost treatment $4,200/month; fees based on patient's ability to pay. Los Angeles County residents not refused treatment due to inability to pay. Fifteen-bed on-site medically monitored detox. Inpatient, outpatient, day treatment, and sober living programs available. The Betty Ford Center has a good relationship with CRI-HELP. Average length of stay for county-funded beds is four to six months, private-pay length of stay based on patient's fund availability. Wait list for males, two to five months; females, one to three months, as of June 1, 2005.

Gateways Beit T'Shuvah

310-204-5200

8831 Venice Boulevard

Los Angeles, CA 90034-3223

www.beittshuvahla.org

Emotional and spiritual healing integrating the Torah and the Twelve Steps for individuals and families afflicted with addiction and behavioral disorders.

Hacienda Valdez

760-329-2959

12890 Quinta Way

Desert Hot Springs, CA 92240

Low-cost sixty-day treatment at $110 per day. Offers five- to seven-day nonmedical detox. Offers transitional housing up to ninety days depending on bed availability. Has Proposition 36 and drug court beds available. This facility is affiliated with The Ranch.

Haight-Ashbury Free Clinics, Inc.

415-565-1908
529 Clayton Street
San Francisco, CA 94117
www.hafci.org

The mission of the Haight-Ashbury Free Clinics, Inc. (HAFCI) is to increase access to health care for all and improve the health and well-being of their clients. The clinics offer low-cost outpatient treatment as well as residential treatment specific to homeless or very low income men, women, and transgender people who are also chronically mentally ill and/or diagnosed with HIV or another serious medical condition, women with HIV/AIDS, and African American men.

Hemet Valley Recovery Center

800-493-0930
951-765-4900
371 Weston Place
Hemet, CA 92543
www.hvrc.com

An acute care primary treatment center offering acute medical detox and specialty services for chronic pain patients and older adults. Able to accept Medicare and most insurance plans for treatment that is determined to be medically appropriate and for most outpatient rehab programs.

Herbert House

877-978-7623

310-737-7566

2531 Sawtelle Boulevard, PMB66

Los Angeles, CA 90064

www.herberthouse.com

Herbert House is located in a quiet residential neighborhood in West Los Angeles, three miles from the beach. Herbert House offers twenty-four-hour management on premises; directors who are trained in the field of chemical dependency and relapse prevention; dedicated leadership with many years of experience; an established drug-free facility with proven principles recognized with deep ties to the recovery community; zero tolerance for substance use; random, weekly drug testing; and in-house meetings. Outside 12-step meetings required. Ninety-day minimum stay recommended. Separate men's and women's houses. The program costs start at $1,800 per month. Eighty percent of rooms are double occupancy.

Hope's Horizon

760-322-1609

4491 Camino San Miquel

Palm Springs, CA 92264

Sober living home for women who have successfully completed a recovery program. Length of stay: four months. Cost: $300/month. Residents are responsible for their own food.

Las Encinas Hospital
800-792-2345

626-795-9901

2900 East Del Mar Boulevard

Pasadena, CA 91107

www.lasencinashospital.com

Las Encinas offers a full range of behavioral health care and chemical dependency treatment options, including inpatient, partial hospitalization, and outpatient services for adolescents and adults.

Loma Linda University Behavioral Medicine Center
800-752-5999

909-558-4425

1710 Barton Road

Redlands, CA 92373

www.llu.edu

Seventh-Day Adventist Medical detox and chemical dependency facility for patients suffering from pain issues. Also offers sober living residence operated by the alumni association.

Matrix Institute
800-310-7700

Greg Allen, Program Director: 310-207-4322

12304 Santa Monica Boulevard, #200

Los Angeles, CA 90025

www.matrixinstitute.org

Outpatient treatment facilities located in Los Angeles, San Fernando Valley,

Rancho Cucamonga, and Costa Mesa. Treatment for adolescents provided at the West Los Angeles and coastal communities. Free outpatient counseling in a research study for meth/speed users at the Costa Mesa location.

Monte Nido

310-457-9958

27612 Sea Vista Drive

Malibu, CA 90265

www.montenido.com

Treatment for women with eating disorders, body image problems, and/or exercise addiction. Lengths of stay range from a minimum of thirty days to four months depending on patient need. Betty Ford Center nutritionist Karen Blachley highly recommends facility.

Montecatini

760-436-8930

2524 La Costa Avenue

Rancho La Costa, CA 92009

www.montecatinieatingdisorder.com

Specializes in the comprehensive care of adolescents and women struggling with anorexia nervosa, bulimia nervosa, binge eating disorder, and other addictions. Program offers residential inpatient, day, and intensive outpatient treatment.

National Alcohol & Drug Treatment Program

310-943-5400

11251 National Boulevard

Los Angeles, CA 90064

www.nationalhealthcarecenters.com

Adult day care center with dual diagnosis/chemical dependency (no detox) and a mental health program geared toward geriatrics. Accepts sliding scale and MediCal.

New Found Life, Inc.
800-635-9899

562-434-4060

562-856-5547

2211 E.ast Ocean Boulevard

Long Beach, CA 90803

www.newfoundlife.com

State-licensed, certified, and court-approved residential treatment center for both men and women recovering from the disease of alcoholism and drug addiction. Primary chemical dependency and extended care facility. New Found Life, Inc. is a court-sentencing alternative, having been approved by courts in Los Angeles and Orange counties. Close professional relationship with the Betty Ford Center. We use them for a continuing care resource, and they send their family members to our family program.

New Directions for Women
800-939-6636

Jan Christie, Executive Director: 949-548-5546

2601 Willow Lane

Costa Mesa, CA 92627

www.newdirectionsforwomen.com

A thirty-bed treatment facility in a residential setting for women 18 and older; twelve-bed residential facility for six women and their dependent children. Programs include inpatient, day-intensive outpatient, work search, and intermediate living levels of care in a highly structured, supportive, and safe environment. Focus of treatment includes recovery, relapse prevention, and life-management skills.

Ohlhoff Recovery Programs (Executive Offices)

415-626-9782 ext. 16
Admitting: 415-626-9782 ext. 21
601 Steiner Street
San Francisco, CA 94117
www.ohlhoff.org

Low-cost inpatient, outpatient, and day treatment for men and women suffering from chemical dependency; six-month extended care treatment for men and outpatient eating disorder treatment for men, women, and adolescents. Various locations throughout the Bay Area.

Rader Programs

800-841-1515
Pacific Shores Hospital
2130 Ventura Road
Oxnard, CA 93030
www.raderprograms.com

Specializing in eating and related disorders, including sexual abuse for men and women. Locations at Pacific Shores Hospital in Oxnard, California, and Brookhaven Hospital in Tulsa, Oklahoma. Levels of care include inpatient, outpatient, day care, continuing care, and family programs. Refers to Betty Ford Center IP services.

The Ranch

760-329-2924

7885 Annandale Avenue

Desert Hot Springs, CA 92240

www.ranchrecovery.org

Low-cost treatment for men. The Ranch has contracts with the county, Proposition 36, Musicians Assistance, Indian Health, and many others. Length of stay varies from 60 to 120 days dependent on patient's need. Also offers transitional partial treatment, partial sober living, and sober living. Nonmedical five- to seven-day detox.

River Community

626-910-1202

23701 East Fork Road

Azusa, CA 91702

www.socialmodel.com

Residential, day treatment, and IOP services for people with concurrent mental health and alcohol and other drug problems. Reasonably priced with financial assistance and partial funding by the Los Angeles County Department of Mental Health and Health Services.

Sober Living by the Sea

800-647-0042

2811 Villa Way

Newport Beach, CA 92263

www.soberliving.com

Ninety-day residential treatment for alcoholism, chemical dependency, and other addictions. Other facilities include Sunrise Recovery Ranch, an all-male, thirty-day facility nestled in the California foothills, and the Victorian House, an all-female, homelike, sixty-day treatment center for eating disorders also located in Newport Beach. Extended care facility. Christian and relapse tracks available; education program available/partnership with local college.

Soroptimist International House of Hope

Banning, CA, ninety days (fully county funded, no cost): 909-849-9491

Desert Hot Springs, CA, ninety days (fully county funded, no cost): 760-329-4673

Palm Springs, CA (reentry program, four months max. $55/wk): 760-322-1609

Extended care, low-cost treatment for women.

The Thelma McMillen Center

3330 Lomita Boulevard
Torrance, CA 90505
Admissions: 310-257-5760

Torrance Memorial Medical Center Business Development

310-784-4879
3333 Skypark Drive, Suite 200
Torrance, CA 90505
www.torrancememorial.org/tmcmillen.htm

Adolescent intensive outpatient substance abuse treatment. The program utilizes individual, group, and family treatment approach using the 12-step philosophy.

Twin Town Treatment Center

562-594-8844
4388 East Katella Avenue

Los Alamitos, CA 90720

www.twintowntreatmentcenters.com

Adolescent (ages 13–17) outpatient day and evening treatment in Los Alamitos, North Hollywood, Orange, and Torrance. Bilingual (Spanish) program available at the Orange location.

Touchstones

714-639-5542

P.O. Box 849

Orange, CA 92856

http://www.socialmodel.com/

Primary chemical dependency available for any child at ninth-grade level and younger than 18; must be willing to participate in voluntary program and free from medical problems. Residential and nonresidential phases available; on-site school available. Sliding scale based on income; many health insurance plans covered; lower rate for Orange County residents. Family encouraged to participate; aftercare support groups and alumni support groups.

UCLA Neuropsychiatric Hospital

800-825-9989

310-825-9989

Los Angeles, CA

www.mentalhealth.ucla.edu/ptcare/

Neuropsychiatric and behavioral disorders treatment for adults, adolescents, and children. Offers specific programs for older adults. Provides inpatient, outpatient, and partial hospitalization programs.

Village Counseling Breaking Free Program

73302 Highway 111, Palm Desert, CA: 760-773-0669

13560 Palm Drive, Desert Hot Springs, CA: 760-288-3123

51800 Harrison Avenue, Coachella, CA: 760-398-8055

A sixteen-week intensive outpatient treatment program for adults and teens struggling with drugs, alcohol, or violence. The program offers individual, group, and family therapy, coupled with case management and strong education components. Proposition 36 funded or affordable sliding scale self-pay.

Visions Adolescent Treatment Center

866-889-3665

33335 Muhlholland Highway

Malibu, CA 90265

www.visionsteen.com

A personalized program dedicated to helping youth and their families recover from the destructive effects of substance use and other behavior-related problems.

Women in Recovery

Sister Ada Garrety, Director/CEO

310-821-6401

911 Coeur D'Alene Avenue

Venice, CA 90291

www.womeninrecovery.com/location.htm

Gender-specific, low-cost, extended care treatment. Strong structure and 12-step orientation. Excellent leadership with a "no-nonsense" approach to treatment. Excellent for those reluctant to recover.

——— **COLORADO** ———

Mile High Council on Alcohol and Drug Abuse

Executive Director, Flavia Lewis, MSW, CACIII

800-537-8098

303-825-8113

1444 Wazee Street, No. 125

Denver, CO 80202

www.milehighcouncil.com

Twenty-four-hour referral, personal response to emergencies, treatment, reference, and 12-step resource. Substance abuse prevention and education resources for teens, adult outpatient services, and gender-specific, culturally sensitive treatment programs for women in Denver County jail.

Valley Hope Information

800-654-0486

Admissions: 800-544-5101

Inpatient program in Parker, CO

Outpatient programs in Colorado Springs, Englewood, and Westminster, CO

www.valleyhope.com

Valley Hope is a nationally recognized, nonprofit organization dedicated to providing quality alcohol and drug addiction treatment services at an affordable price. Their individualized treatment plans are based on the 12-step philosophy with a strong emphasis on family participation, spirituality (nondenominational), and continuing care. Valley Hope operates IP and IOP treatment facilities in seven states: Arizona, Colorado, Kansas, Missouri, Nebraska, Oklahoma, and Texas.

FLORIDA

Advanced Recovery Center

877-272-4673

561-274-7417

1300 Park of Commerce Boulevard, #200

Delray Beach, FL 33445

www.arc-hope.com

Gender-relevant residential, extended care, and transitional treatment for dual diagnosis and eating disorders designed to address critical, unresolved issues that are likely to lead patients into chronic relapse. Will allow patients to bring their pets (up to twenty-five pounds).

Hanley Center

800-444-7008

561-841-1000

5200 East Avenue

West Palm Beach, FL 33407

www.hanleycenter.org

Twelve-step–based treatment program designed to address the specific needs of the older adult. Minimum length of stay: twenty-eight days; cost: $22,300 (includes medical detox; does not include medications). Does not take Medicare or Medicaid.

Transitions Recovery Program

800-626-1980

305-949-9001

1928 N.E. 154th Street, Suite 100

North Miami Beach, FL 33162

www.transrecovery.com

Reasonably priced chemical dependency treatment and licensed behavioral healthcare provider. Offers a freestanding residential recovery program as well as partial day and outpatient treatment.

Turning Point of Tampa, Inc.
800-397-3006
813-882-3003
5439 Beaumont Center Boulevard, #1010
Tampa, FL 33634
www.tpoftampa.com

Inpatient and outpatient eating disorder treatment based on a holistic approach while adhering to a 12-step philosophy. Discounted rates for self-pay.

Wellness Resource Center
800-455-7483
7940 N. Federal Highway
Boca Raton, FL 33487
www.wellnessresourcecenter.com

Wellness Resource Center provides affordable treatment for individuals suffering from dual diagnosis of psychiatric illness and chemical dependency.

———— ILLINOIS ————

Hazelden Chicago
800-257-7810
1919 S. Highland Avenue, Lombard, IL: 630-424-7280
1121 Lake Cook Road, Deerfield, IL: 847-405-0697
http://www.hazelden.org/

Youth and family outpatient treatment. Also offers an educational program for teens who have experienced negative consequences due to drug or alcohol use but are not in need of treatment. Program can be an alternative to school suspension.

Rosecrance on Harrison

815-391-1000

3815 Harrison Avenue

Rockford, IL 61108

Julie Clayton, Assessment and Admissions Coordinator

www.rosecrance.org

Rosecrance on Harrison is an adult, gender-specific IP and IOP program that offers primary chemical dependency treatment. They do work with managed care companies and cost approximately $14,000 for thirty days. Included in the cost is their family program for all family members wishing to participate. They do not offer a financial assistance program (FAP) but will work out payment plans.

Rosecrance Griffin Williamson Campus

Marcia Maggio, Assessment and Admissions Coordinator

815-391-1000

1601 University Drive

Rockford, IL 61107

www.rosecrance.org

Treatment for adolescents ages 12–19 with IP, IOP, and an on-site school offered. They work with managed care companies and cost approximately $17,000 for thirty days. Included in the cost is their family program for all family members wishing to participate. They do offer a financial assistance program (FAP) and will work out payment plans. In addition, they offer off-campus housing for young women ages 15–19 who are able to attend high school or college in the area. The cost for this program is $45,000 for the year. This is a long-term treatment program ranging from three months to two years.

———•—— **KANSAS** ——•———

Valley Hope

800-654-0486

Admissions: 800-544-5101

Inpatient programs in Atchison, Halstead (hospital-based program), and
  Norton, KS

Outpatient programs in Mission and Wichita, KS

www.valleyhope.com

Valley Hope is a nationally recognized, nonprofit organization dedicated to
providing quality alcohol and drug addiction treatment services at an affordable
price. Their individualized treatment plans are based on the 12-step philosophy
with a strong emphasis on family participation, spirituality (nondenominational), and continuing care. Valley Hope operates IP and IOP treatment facilities
in seven states: Arizona, Colorado, Kansas, Missouri, Nebraska, Oklahoma, and
Texas.

———•—— **LOUISIANA** ——•———

The Journey Home Recovery Center, Inc.

504-644-0185

206 North Irma Boulevard

Gonzales, LA 70737

www.thejourneyhome.com

Low-cost chemical dependency, abuse, and/or dual diagnosis treatment for
adolescent females 14 years and older. Open-ended, extended care treatment
offering social and medical detox.

River Oaks Psychiatric
800-366-1740
504-734-1740
1525 River Oaks Road West
New Orleans, LA 70123
www.riveroakshospital.com

Private psychiatric facility for adults, adolescents, and children for the treatment of acute psychiatric illness, dual diagnosis, trauma-based disorders, eating disorders, and compulsive behaviors.

St. Christopher's
Dwayne Beason: cell 225-975-0216
Baton Rouge, LA
Excellent resource for young men ages 17 and older.

―――― MARYLAND ――――

Father Martin's Ashley House
800-799-4673
410-273-6600
800 Tydings Lane
Havre de Grace, MD 21078
www.fathermartinsashley.com

Nondenominational, nonprofit center for the treatment of alcoholics and chemically dependent people. Also offers an inpatient relapse program.

—•— MINNESOTA —•—

The Gables

800-422-5370

604 5th Street, S.W.

Rochester, MN 55902

Licensed thirty-bed extended care facility for the treatment of chemically dependent women ages 15 and over. Offers concurrent treatment to women with anorexia, bulimia, or atypical eating patterns. Also offers dual diagnosis treatment.

Hazelden Center for Youth and Family

800-257-7810

763-509-3800

11505 36th Avenue, North

Plymouth, MN 55441-2398

www.hazelden.org

Alcoholism and drug dependency treatment services to youth ages 14–25. Full range of primary care services including outpatient and residential extended care services.

Hazelden Women and Children's Recovery Community

800-257-7810

New Brighton, MN

http://www.hazelden.org/

Fifteen one- and two-bedroom apartments for newly sober, chemically dependent women, particularly single mothers with children. Services such as individual, group, and family support in addition to weekly home visits and facilities for 12-step meetings provided. Living skills and social reintegration needs also addressed.

Hazelden: Your Next Step Tobacco Cessation Program

800-257-7810

651-213-4000

15245 Pleasant Valley Road

Center City, MN 55012

www.hazelden.org (Services/Tobacco Recovery)

Seven-day holistic approach—mind, body, and spirit—to quitting tobacco.

Mayo Clinic/Rochester Methodist Hospital (St. Mary's Hospital)

Kathy Riekel: 507-255-3636

1216 2nd Street, Southwest

Generose Building, 1st Floor East

Rochester, MN 55902

Chemical dependency with medical complications and/or psychiatric issues. Average length of stay ten to fourteen days, then patient is transferred to either intensive outpatient program at Mayo or treatment local to the patient.

Please visit www.scottmdavis.blogspot.com
for further information and discussion on addiction and recovery.

Pride Institute

800-547-7433

14400 Martin Drive

Eden Prairie, MN 55344

www.pride-institute.com

Dual diagnosis treatment for gay, lesbian, bisexual, and transgender people. Treatment facilities in Fort Lauderdale, Florida; Chicago, Illinois; Dallas–Fort Worth, Texas; and New York City, New York. Medicare accepted.

—·— MISSISSIPPI —·—

Pine Grove Next Step

601-288-2273

Toll Free Nationwide: 800-321-8750

Toll Free in Mississippi: 800-821-7399

2253 Broadway Drive

Hattiesburg, MS 39402

http://www.nextstep-treatment.com/

Pine Grove's Chemical Dependency Unit offers a variety of 12-step–based programs, including inpatient, outpatient, and day treatment. Our interdisciplinary staff of physicians, nurses, counselors, clinical assistants, social workers, and a certified addictionologist provide patients with a full continuum of care. Dual diagnosis and adolescents. Works with Blue Cross and Medicare/Medicaid.

———•— MISSOURI —•———

Valley Hope Information

800-654-0486

Admissions: 800-544-5101

Inpatient program in Boonville, MO

Outpatient programs in Boonville, Springfield, and St. Louis
(all in Missouri)

www.valleyhope.com

Valley Hope is a nationally recognized nonprofit organization dedicated to providing quality alcohol and drug addiction treatment services at an affordable price. Their individualized treatment plans are based on the 12-step philosophy with a strong emphasis on family participation, spirituality (nondenominational), and continuing care. Valley Hope operates IP and IOP treatment facilities in seven states: Arizona, Colorado, Kansas, Missouri, Nebraska, Oklahoma, and Texas.

———•— MONTANA —•———

Wilderness Treatment Program

406-854-2832

200 Hubbart Dam Road

Marion, MT 59925

www.wildernessaltschool.com

Treatment program for chemically addicted adolescents and young adults. Treatment consists of traditional 12-step philosophies in addition to a twenty-one-day Outward Bound–type program.

—•— NEBRASKA —•—

Valley Hope
800-654-0486
Admissions: 800-544-5101
www.valleyhope.com

Valley Hope is a nationally recognized nonprofit organization dedicated to providing quality alcohol and drug addiction treatment services at an affordable price. Their individualized treatment plans are based on the 12-step philosophy with a strong emphasis on family participation, spirituality (nondenominational), and continuing care. Valley Hope operates IP and IOP treatment facilities in seven states: Arizona, Colorado, Kansas, Missouri, Nebraska, Oklahoma, and Texas.

—•— NEVADA —•—

Las Vegas Recovery Center
Michael S. Levy, D.O., FASAM, Medical Director
Brad Boman, Executive Director
800-790-0091
702-515-1373
3371 N. Buffalo Drive
Las Vegas, NV 89129-6283
www.fountainridgelv.com

State-of-the-art medically managed withdrawal facility providing twenty-four-hour medically directed evaluation and withdrawal management in an acute care inpatient setting. Services are delivered under a defined set of physician-approved policies and physician-managed procedures or medical protocol.

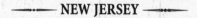

———— NEW JERSEY ————

Alina Lodge
800-575-6343
908-362-6114
Box G
Blairstown, NJ 07825
www.alinalodge.org

Sixty-bed, long-term residential facility for chemically dependent men and women 18 and older. Excellent for the reluctant to recover. Length of stay based on individual need. Average length of stay is five to eight months. Stringent, highly structured treatment protocol.

———— NEW MEXICO ————

The Life Healing Center of Santa Fe
800-989-7406
505-989-7436
P.O. Box 6758
Santa Fe, NM 87502
www.life-healing.com

Therapeutic residential facility specializing in the treatment of adults who have experienced severe emotional trauma ranging from a single traumatic event to ongoing physical, sexual, or emotional abuse. Continuing care offered for eating disorders and relationship difficulties.

Vista Taos
800-245-8267
P.O. Box 978
Taos, NM 87571
www.vistataos.com

Primary and extended care treatment for early childhood trauma, co-dependency, addictive relationships, and eating disorders. Twelve-bed facility offering highly individualized treatment.

——— NEW YORK ———

Hazelden New York
800-257-7810
212-420-9522
233 East 17th Street
New York, NY 10003-3635
http://www.hazelden.org/

Intensive outpatient chemical dependency treatment for adults.

———·— NORTH CAROLINA ——·—

Pavillon International

800-392-4808

500 Pavillon Place

P.O. Box 189

Mill Spring, NC 28756

www.pavillon.org

Four-week closed group treatment for thirty patients per session. Treatment provided for substance abuse, core addiction—codependency, sex and/or relationship addiction, eating disorders, workaholism, compulsive gambling—disorders co-occurring with anxiety, panic attacks, depression, posttraumatic stress disorder, and abuse—sexual, physical, emotional, and religious.

——·— OKLAHOMA ——·—

Valley Hope Information

800-654-0486

Admissions: 800-544-5101

Inpatient program in Cushing, OK

Outpatient program in Oklahoma City and Tulsa, OK

www.valleyhope.com

Valley Hope is a nationally recognized nonprofit organization dedicated to providing quality alcohol and drug addiction treatment services at an affordable price. Their individualized treatment plans are based on the 12-step philosophy with a strong emphasis on family participation, spirituality (nondenominational), and continuing care. Valley Hope operates IP and IOP treatment facilities in seven states: Arizona, Colorado, Kansas, Missouri, Nebraska, Oklahoma, and Texas.

OREGON

Serenity Lane Health Services National

800-543-9905

In Oregon: 800-826-9285

541-687-1110

616 E. 16th Avenue

Eugene, OR 97401

www.serenitylane.org

Moderately priced inpatient, outpatient, and extended care treatment.

PENNSYLVANIA

Caron Foundation

800-678-2332

Galen Hall Road

Wernersville, PA 19565

www.caron.org

Located near Redding, sixty miles west of Philadelphia. Inpatient, outpatient, and extended care for adults and adolescents. Also offers nicotine cessation groups, compulsive eating treatment, codependency treatment, and life enrichment workshops for adults.

Cumberland Heights Residential and OP Services

800-646-9998

Administration: 615-352-1757

Intake, local: 615-356-2700

Cumberland Heights Mobile Assessment Services (24 hours): 615-356-2700

8283 River Road

Nashville, TN 37209

www.cumberlandheights.org

Residential treatment ranging from eight to twenty-eight days, outpatient, women's programs, and youth programs for young men and women ages 13–21.

------ SOUTH CAROLINA ------

Hilton Head Health Institute

843-785-7292

14 Valencia Road

Hilton Head, SC 29928

www.hhhealth.com

Spa environment providing an array of services to encourage a healthy lifestyle. Programs are designed to provide an ideal balance of structured learning and experiential activities. Specific guest goals include weight loss, increasing energy and stamina, lowering cholesterol and blood pressure levels, managing stress more effectively, quitting smoking, and generally feeling better, both physically and emotionally.

—•— **TEXAS** —•—

The Menninger Clinic
800-351-9058
713-275-5000
2801 Gessner
Houston, TX 77080
www.menningerclinic.com

Psychiatric treatment for people of all ages. Continuum of care includes acute hospital services, residential treatment services for people ages 12–18, day treatment services, partial hospitalization services, supportive living program, and specialized services, including treatment for eating disorders, trauma, senior services, multiple personality disorder, sleep disorders, and others. Also offering a new specialty hospital for dual diagnosis treatment of young adults ages 18–30 experiencing difficulty transitioning from adolescence to adulthood and seeking treatment for a psychiatric disorder co-occurring with an addiction disorder.

Nexus Recovery Center, Inc.
214-321-0156
8733 La Prada Drive
Dallas, TX 75228
www.nexusrecovery.org

Nonprofit residential and outpatient substance abuse facility for women, women with children, and adolescent girls. Childcare services offered for clients when they are in group. Can handle same-day admissions.

Valley Hope

800-654-0486

Admissions: 800-544-5101

Inpatient program in Grapevine, TX

Outpatient program in Garland, Grapevine, and Lake Worth, TX

www.valleyhope.com

Valley Hope is a nationally recognized nonprofit organization dedicated to providing quality alcohol and drug addiction treatment services at an affordable price. Their individualized treatment plans are based on the 12-step philosophy with a strong emphasis on family participation, spirituality (nondenominational), and continuing care. Valley Hope operates IP and IOP treatment facilities in seven states: Arizona, Colorado, Kansas, Missouri, Nebraska, Oklahoma, and Texas.

 UTAH

Aspen Education Group

800-283-8334

General questions: Debbie Hopper: 949-495-6115

P.O. Box 400

Loa, UT 84747

www.aspeneducation.com

Fully accredited, professionally supervised outdoor therapy program for adolescents ages 13–17. Specializes in working with adolescents with behavioral problems, substance abuse problems, and/or educational difficulties. The Wilderness Program was recently expanded to include young adults.

Cirque Lodge

800-582-0709

801-222-9200

RR 3 Box A-10

Sundance, UT 84604

www.cirquelodge.com

Sixteen-bed primary chemical dependency facility. Surrounding lends itself to a spiritual experience, excellent for the reluctant to recover. Excellent facility for active adults. Treats drug dependency as long as the chemical dependency is primary. Private rooms available.

Provo Canyon School

800-848-9819

801-227-2000

4501 N. University Avenue

Provo, UT 84603

www.provocanyon.com

Secured, 211-bed residential treatment facility specializing in behavioral health services for boys and girls ages 12–17 who have capacity for normal functioning but are manifesting emotional, behavioral, and learning difficulties and have been unresponsive to outpatient counseling or previous inpatient psychiatric or substance abuse programs. Continuum of care includes individual, group, family, and experiential therapy.

—••— WASHINGTON —••—

Gray Wolf Ranch

800-571-5501

360-385-5505

P.O. Box 102

Port Townsend, WA 98368

www.graywolfranch.com

Intermediate care residential recovery lodge, providing a transitional living environment for up to twenty-four young men between the ages of 14–25 in early recovery from chemical dependency. Candidates for Gray Wolf must be sober thirty days through primary treatment.

Sundown M Ranch

800-326-7444

509-457-0990

2280 SR 221, P.O. Box 217

Yakima, WA 98901

www.sundown.org

Low-cost, primary chemical dependency treatment for adults and adolescents (grades 4–12). Also offers Elder Groups for men and women 50+ years of age as well as inpatient, outpatient, and family programs.

———•— WEST VIRGINIA —•———

Alldredge Academy
888-468-1828
P.O. Box 310, William Avenue
Davis, WV 26260
www.alldredgeacademy.org

The Alldredge Academy is a fully accredited coed school/program for adolescents ages 13–18. Alldredge is designed to be a short-term school/program moving beyond wilderness therapy to open doors of learning and change in four distinct environments. Highly recommended by Bill Maher.

———•— BILINGUAL/INTERNATIONAL —•———

Asian-American Drug Abuse Program
323-293-6284
5318 Crenshaw Boulevard
Los Angeles, CA 90043
www.aadapinc.ws

Treatment services provided for people throughout Los Angeles County. Outpatient, day treatment, drug court treatment program, and HIV/AIDS street outreach and case management. Also offers extended care (twelve to eighteen months) treatment providing individual, group, and family counseling, psychosocial assessment, individual treatment planning, access to basic medical, dental, and legal services, work therapy, social and recreational activities, educational seminars, GED courses, and job search.

ASK Human Care, Inc.
Tsukasa Mizusawa: 011-81-3-3249-2551
SOGNO 21, Bldg. 3-19-3
NIHOMBASHI-HAMACHO, CHUO-KU, TOKYO 103-0007
Email: ask@t3.rim.or.jp
www.t3.or.jp/~ask/

Bellwood Health Services, Inc.
800-387-6198
416-495-0926
1020 McNichol Avenue
Scarborough, Ontario
Canada M1W 2J6
www.bellwood.ca

Treatment for people with alcohol and drug addictions, eating disorders, gambling and sexual addictions, stress-related illnesses, and a variety of compulsive or problematic behaviors.

Caritas Counseling Services
760-674-9066
909-370-1293
73-441 Fred Waring Drive
Palm Desert, CA 92260
1265 N. La Cadena, Suite 4
Colton, CA 92324

Low-cost outpatient individual and family counseling services. Bilingual, Spanish.

Casa Las Palmas
760-347-9442
83844 Hopi Avenue
Indio, CA 92201
E-mail: Casalaspalmas@aol.com

Spanish-speaking, no-cost, primary chemical dependency six-bed facility. Length of stay is ninety days. Will make referrals to other Spanish-speaking programs.

Catholic Charities
909-388-1239
1450 North D Street
San Bernardino, CA 92405

Low-cost outpatient individual and family counseling services.

Hacienda Del Lago/Mexico
011-52-376-6-1457
Ajijic, Jalisco, Mexico
http://www.lahacienda.com/

Treatment program specifically designed for the Spanish-speaking individual. Facility mirrors philosophy and therapeutic modalities of La Hacienda in Hunt, Texas (medical services and detox, adult chemical dependency programs, and family program).

International Rehabilitation Centers, Inc.
011-527-120-1511
www.jamaicarehab.com

Private, exclusive recovery treatment centers with luxurious settings located in Cuernavaca, Mexico, Negril, and Jamaica. Specializing in chemical dependency, adolescent treatment, treatment for depression, eating disorders, abuse and trauma healing, behavioral treatment, and dual diagnosis treatment. Private rooms available.

Oceanica
011-52-669-989-8800
Priory Healthcare: 020-8876-8261
www.oceanica.com.mx

Roehampton Priory
Priory Lane, Roehampton
London, England SW15 5JJ
www.prioryhealthcare.co.uk/roehampton

Offers treatment for all aspects of acute psychiatric conditions, including depression and schizophrenia, with special programs for the treatment of eating disorders, alcoholism, drug abuse, and anxiety-related disorders. Inpatient, outpatient, and day patient programs on a one-to-one or group basis are individually tailored to the patient's needs and preferences, and a wide variety of approaches are used, including cognitive and behavioral therapies. Treatment programs are offered for depression, alcohol/drug misuse, posttraumatic stress disorders, eating disorders, postnatal depression and mother and baby, sexual dysfunction, bereavement, obsessive compulsive disorders, phobias, anxiety problems, family problems, and marital problems.

Victory Gruppen Kvarnlyckan
08-765 62 00
Box 1011
Oskarshemmet 08-767 00 90
181 21 Lidingo

———•— HELPLINES/HOTLINES —•———

Angel Step Inn hotline: 323-780-4357
Walk-in resource center: 562-949-5358
P.O. Box 689
Downey, CA 90241
9423 Slauson Avenue
Pico Rivera, CA
Domestic violence hotline and resource center.

California Council on Compulsive Gambling, Inc.
From within California: 800-322-8748
From outside California: 800-522-4700
121 South Palm Canyon Drive, Suite 225
Palm Springs, CA 92262

California Poison Control System: 800-876-4766

California Smokers Helpline: 800-766-2888

Coachella Valley Sexual Assault Services 24-hour Crisis Line: 760-568-9071
Free counseling for rape and adults molested as children (AMAC) survivors.
    Free groups for AMAC.

Coast to Coast Drug and Alcohol Referral Service: 800-616-9998
Executive Director: Kirby Dean: 949-766-5753
General referrals to low-cost, no-cost treatment.

Covenant House NINELINE: 800-999-9999
Crisis intervention, referral/info services for troubled teens and families.

Desert Aids Project
81893 Carreon Boulevard, Indio, CA: 760-342-4197
1695 North Sunrise Way, Palm Springs, CA: 760-323-2118

National Aids Hotline: 800-342-2437

National Alcohol and Drug Abuse Hotline: 800-252-6465
Referral service for alcohol and drug abuse facilities.

National Clearinghouse for Alcohol and Drug Information (NCADI):
    800-729-6686

National Council on Alcoholism and Drug Dependence (NCADD):
    212-269-7797
20 Exchange Place, #2902
New York, NY 10005-3201

National Institute on Drug Abuse (NIDA)
www.drugabuse.gov

National Runaway Switchboard: 800-621-4000
Hotline for runaway and homeless youth and their families.

New Directions/C.A.R.E. at Park Cities YMCA
214-526-8986
6000 Preston Road
Dallas, TX 75205
www.pcymca.org

Office of Substance Abuse Prevention (OSAP)

P.O. Box 2345

Rockville, MD 20847-2345

Alcohol and drug information and referrals.

Recovery Options Network: 800-662-2873

(You should reach a counselor until 6:00 PM. If you reach an answering
   machine, leave a message and a counselor will be paged immediately.)

32234 Paseo Adelanto, Suite C

San Juan Capistrano, CA 92675

Associated with Pacific Hills Treatment Center, they can provide you with
   information on that program. Service should provide you with three
   options for treatment; please call back if you do not feel the service is
   able to meet your needs.

Riverside County Department of Mental Health: 800-472-4305

Suicide Prevention Hotline, Rape Crisis Center

Shelter of the Storm: 760-328-7233

Southern California Alcohol and Drug Programs: 562-494-7709

Next Step Job and Career Center

2725 E. Pacific Coast Highway, Suite 202

Long Beach, CA 90804

Job skills class, career planning, computer training, and so on.

State of California AIDS Drug Assistance Program: 888-311-7632

433 Callan Avenue, Suite 207

San Leandro, CA 94577

Assistance with access to HIV-related prescription drugs; continuation of
   private health insurance.

Substance Abuse and Mental Health Services Administration (SAMHSA):
   800-662-4357
www.samhsa.gov
Online chemical dependency facility locator service; 24-hour hotline.

Teen Help Adolescent Referrals: 800-400-0900
Refers struggling teens to long-term residential programs.

Youth Crisis Hotline: 800-448-4663
Counseling and referrals for teens in crisis.

Appendix 3: Self-Assessment Questionnaire Screening for Alcohol, Drug, or Behavioral Addiction or Abuse

*F*ollowing is a self-assessment questionnaire to help you decide if you or someone you care about has a problem with a substance or behavioral addiction or abuse. Answer these questions as honestly as you can. You may wish to discuss the results with a professional experienced in dealing with addiction, an alcoholic/addict in a recovery program, or someone else you trust.

1. What are the substance(s) or behavior(s) that you are concerned about possibly being addicted to?

2. When did you start using or engaging in it (them), and for how long?

3. How much, and how often, do you use the substance(s) or participate in the behavior(s)?

For the following questions, consider the last twelve months:

4. Has this substance or behavior affected your physical health? ❑ Yes ❑ No

5. Has this substance or behavior affected
   your thinking patterns, concentration,
   or attitude?   ❏ Yes ❏ No

6. Has this substance or behavior affected
   your mood or feelings?   ❏ Yes ❏ No

7. Has this substance or behavior affected
   your personality?   ❏ Yes ❏ No

8. Has this substance or behavior affected
   your self-esteem?   ❏ Yes ❏ No

9. Has this substance or behavior negatively
   affected your job or school performance?   ❏ Yes ❏ No

10. Has this substance or behavior negatively
    affected your financial condition?   ❏ Yes ❏ No

11. Has this substance or behavior negatively
    affected your relationships with your
    family, including your children?   ❏ Yes ❏ No

12. Has this substance or behavior created
    legal problems?   ❏ Yes ❏ No

13. Has this substance or behavior negatively
    affected your religious beliefs and/or
    your spirituality?   ❏ Yes ❏ No

14. Has a family member, friend, or co-
    worker expressed concern over your
    possible addictive use of a substance or
    involvement in an addictive behavior?   ❏ Yes ❏ No

SCORING AND ASSESSMENT

Review your responses to the self-assessment questionnaire and total the number of "yes" responses. Using Appendices 4A and 4B as a guide, note that *three or more "yes" responses* to these questions indicates a likely pattern of addiction to alcohol, drugs, or a compulsive behavior that may necessitate treatment.

Answering "yes" to *at least one of the questions* indicates a likely pattern of substance abuse. Substance abuse *may* require less intensive treatment than a substance or behavioral addiction. However, substance abuse can be the forerunner to the increasingly destructive substance dependence if not quickly controlled by therapeutic intervention.

If you or someone you care about meets the criteria for an addiction (dependence) or substance abuse problem, consult the resource lists in this book to find help for further treatment or additional information.

Appendix 4A: Diagnostic Criteria for Chemical Dependence[1]

A maladaptive pattern of substance use, leading to clinically significant impairment or distress, as manifested by three or more of the following occurring at any time in the same twelve-month period:

1. Tolerance, as defined by either of the following:
   (a) A need for markedly increased amounts of the substance to achieve intoxication or desired effect.
   (b) Markedly diminished effect with continued use of the same amount of the substance.

2. Withdrawal, as manifested by either of the following:
   (a) The characteristic withdrawal syndrome for the substance.
   (b) The same (or a closely related) substance is taken to relieve or avoid withdrawal symptoms.

3. The substance is often taken in larger amounts or over a longer period than was intended.

---

[1] *The American Psychiatric Association,* Diagnostic and Statistical Manual of Mental Disorders, *4th ed., text rev. (Washington, DC: American Psychiatric Association, 2000).*

4. There is a persistent desire or unsuccessful efforts to cut down or control use.

5. A great deal of time is spent in activities necessary to obtain the substance (e.g., visiting multiple doctors or driving long distances), use the substance (e.g., chain-smoking), or recover from its effects.

6. Important social, occupational, or recreational activities are given up or reduced because of substance use.

7. The substance use is continued despite knowledge of having a persistent or recurrent physical or psychological problem that is likely to have been caused or exacerbated by the substance (e.g., current cocaine use despite recognition of cocaine-induced depression, or continued drinking despite recognition that an ulcer was made worse by alcohol consumption).

Appendix 4B: Diagnostic Criteria for Substance Abuse[1]

A maladaptive pattern of substance use leading to clinically significant impairment or distress, as manifested by one or more of the following occurring within a twelve-month period:

1. Recurrent substance use resulting in a failure to fulfill major role obligations at work, school, or home (e.g., repeated absences or poor work performance related to substance use; substance-related absences, suspensions, or expulsions from school; neglect of children or household).

2. Recurrent substance use in situations in which it is physically hazardous (e.g., driving an automobile or operating a machine when impaired by substance use).

3. Recurrent substance-related legal problems (e.g., arrests for substance-related disorderly conduct).

---

1 *The American Psychiatric Association,* Diagnostic and Statistical Manual of Mental Disorders, 4th ed., text rev. (*Washington, DC: American Psychiatric Association, 2000*).

4. Continued substance use despite having persistent or recurrent social or interpersonal problems caused or exacerbated by the effects of the substance (e.g., arguments with spouse about consequences of intoxication, physical fights).

Appendix 5A: Intervention Resources for Alcohol and Drug Addiction/Abuse

I. INTRODUCTION

*T*he greatest problem with drug or alcohol abusers is that they usually do not know they are out of control. They look around and make comparisons with other abusers and argue that they are normal. These people need objective and honest feedback on their behavior. Motivation of a skilled counselor and the support of family and friends can help a person realize the situation. The process that helps an addict recognize the gravity of his problem is called intervention.

Many believe that a drug abuser can only get better if he is self-motivated to change. This is an outdated idea. A skilled professional can motivate an abuser toward recovery at any stage of addiction. In fact, intervention is the best way to provide help to those struggling with addiction. It is a nonjudgmental, noncritical, systematic process that makes an addict come to terms with the impact of his alcoholism or drug use on others.

Getting the addict to seek treatment as early as possible is the main, if not the only, purpose of intervention. But this can be a challenging situation. You cannot force an abuser, under *most* circumstances, to undergo treatment. At the same time, you cannot afford things getting worse. Experts suggest many ways to overcome this dilemma, like training ourselves to stop protecting the abuser from the consequences of his behavior and leaving him no choice but to seek treatment.

If intervention is done by someone the addict particularly trusts, it has a greater chance of being successful. This can be a family member, a close friend, or anyone concerned enough to help the addict. A professional counselor with a good reputation can play an effective role in intervention. At a meeting in the presence of a counselor, the addict's family and friends can express their concerns about the addict and his/her behavior. They can speak up about their decision that they will no longer tolerate the addiction. If they are able to convince the addict, with the help of the counselor, and make him seek treatment for his behavior, the intervention can be considered successful.

Conducting a drug intervention is a complicated and delicate matter. Addicts are in a special kind of mental state and trust no one. They believe that the whole world is against them. So, they may feel cornered and become more defensive. This makes the determination of a proper strategy and timing for intervention very important. The presence of a professional counselor is very helpful in these situations.

What Is an Intervention?

Addiction intervention is the step that comes before a person enters the recovery program. A loving get-together, an alcohol/drug intervention is about letting the addict realize that the problems hounding him are due to his habit and the ill effects his habit has on his family. Just the fact that all his loved ones have gathered with one purpose, experiencing the love flowing, will be enough to make any substance abuser realize the need for him to get into recovery. Once he realizes that all of them care for him and want him to get better, he has taken the first step to realizing his self-worth. He has to realize that he has so many people loving him for what he is, and that he is the luckiest person in the world because of this. The addict must recognize the fact that he has an addiction. It is usually some sort of crisis—a car accident, DUI, or even a complete memory loss for days—that leads family and friends to talk to the addict about seeking alcohol/drug treatment. Having a trained professional counselor to work with the family and the abuser often guarantees that the abuser will admit to wanting to go for alcohol/drug rehab.

History

Vernon Johnson, who published the book *I'll Quit Tomorrow* in 1973, started experimenting with the technique of intervention as early as the 1960s. This technique was and continues to be the standard against which all further developments are compared and measured. Johnson's book includes the fundamental rationale and approach to interventions still used today. There have been many developments in this field over the last few decades. People began to recognize that the intervention technique was applicable to a wide range of situations and issues. The tremendous advancements in the techniques and the growing influence of drugs have substantially increased the acceptance of intervention since Vernon Johnson first articulated his thoughts.

Is Intervention Necessary?

There are many people who are under the mistaken belief
that no intervention can be successful in the long run, because
most addicts can't be helped until they are ready to reach out
for help on their own. In fact, only a small percentage of substance abusers recover without intervention. For the majority,
assistance is inevitable. In fact, intervention is an indispensa-
ble part of the healing process. Along with the dependence on
a substance comes a reluctance to tackle the problem. Addicts
often use "denial" as their defense mechanism. Conceit and
ego also play their parts in denying addiction. Breaking this
defense is the first step in the process of intervention. It is
imperative that intervention be done safely and with confiden-
tiality. The advice and counsel of an experienced, trained, and
certified professional interventionist are essential. The interventionist must be knowledgeable in the right approach or
treatment methodology. He needs to work in cooperation with
the family of the addict.

The Right Time for Intervention

What is the right time for an intervention? The answer is obvious—as soon as an alcohol or drug addiction problem has been
identified. Consultation with a treatment professional or intervention specialist will help you determine whether the addict
needs an intervention. Professional intervention is not a choice
for everyone and every situation. As most cases do not require
a full intervention, this consultation bears great significance.

The process of intervention can be as long as several weeks
to as short as one day. If the situation does not demand an
immediate action, more planning is always appropriate.

The Role of Family and Friends

The role the family and friends of an addict have to play in intervention is vital. Even when they are tired of trying various attempts to control the behavior of the addict, family members tend to protect him/her from the consequences. Stopping such rescue missions is an important part of intervention. The addict needs to fully experience the harmful effects of addiction.

Making the effort a collective one is also very important. Try to find strength in numbers with the help of family and friends, and confront the abuser as a group, but be careful with the words. Assigning one person to talk with the abuser will be much more effective than it would be for everyone to talk at once.

Brief Interventions

The aim of a brief intervention is to motivate the abuser to change his/her problematic behavior. It may include educating the addict on the effects of drinking or drugs and establishing goals and a contract for a change in behavior. Trained clinicians, healthcare workers, social workers, or professional counselors can conduct brief interventions. These interventions can even be done at home.

Pretreatment Interventions

If brief interventions don't help, an abuser needs to undergo a pretreatment intervention. It is a more detailed and longer version of the brief one. Generally, a professional counselor meets with the family before the session to gather facts. This session can be helpful to both parties. The counselor, equipped with all the essential information, can effectively handle the addict. And the family can make necessary changes in their behavior to the addict in accordance with the progression of the intervention.

The main part of pretreatment interventions is the face-to-face sessions with the addict. Normally, a couple of sessions are needed. But, sometimes, as per the requirement, the number of sessions can be five or more.

Will an Intervention Make the Situation Worse?

Normally, a professionally conducted intervention is a gentle, conversational process. It is not an argument or an examination of wills. An intervention is designed to improve the lives and awareness of all involved. Moreover, people who quit without expert assistance usually end up back on drugs or alcohol. So, given the great gains, intervention is something worth trying.

Motivational Interviewing

In 1991, William Miller and Stephen Rollnick challenged the view that all addicts had an intrinsic system of denial. They proposed that techniques by counselors to elicit reactions produced those that they labeled as abnormal and symptomatic of a chemical dependency. Therefore, they suggested that the behavior of the counselor contributes to resistance and denial in the addict. As an alternative, Miller and Rollnick proposed a methodological approach that determined the stages of change in the addict and prescribed the counselor's appropriate course of action. The most important point of motivational interviewing is that the "addict's resistance is a therapist problem." Their point of view, then, is that professionals must change their behavior according to that of the addict.

Failures

An intervention that is perfectly planned and carried out properly will certainly result in an addict's agreeing to accept help. But there is always a chance that the opposite may occur—the addict may, for whatever reason, reject an intervention. If an intervention fails, the situation will most likely get worse. Since everything is out in the open, the message the family gives the abuser at this point is crucial. By not seeking rehab, the addict is telling his family that he would rather continue to use drugs, and that the family will continue to suffer because of this choice.

Even a successful intervention does not guarantee recovery from addiction. Many people consider intervention a failure if the addict does not make the essential transitions during and after formal treatment. But past records show that up to 85 percent of addicted people who underwent intervention sought treatment. This reveals that professionally conducted interventions often achieve their goal, that is, make people willing to seek treatment.

II. Goals of Intervention

Bringing addicts to treatment remained the main goal of alcohol/drug interventions for a long time, but having undergone a vast change in the present, the contemporary aim of addiction intervention is to get the substance abuser to see the larger perspective of the quandary caused by his dependency. It offers resolutions for not just the drug or alcohol abuser but also his loved ones, who are victims of his bad habit. Treating substance abuse is not just about treating the addict but is also about rebuilding those lives that have been destroyed due to the dependency.

Four Main Intervention Goals:

1. **To realize the nature and degree of substance abuse and the focus of the level of treatment and interventions.** An addict often compares himself to his peers and comes to the conclusion that he is normal. As a result, he never realizes that he has lost control due to his alcohol/drug abuse. What he needs in this condition is objective and honest feedback on his behavior. A skilled counselor, with the support of family and friends of the addict, can help him realize the situation through the process of alcohol/drug intervention. The interventionist, who gets an idea of the nature and degree of the addiction through meetings with the addict and family, can make constructive opinions on the addict's behavior. This, to a great extent, may help the addict realize the actual situation.

A drug or alcohol intervention is a bid to help, with the clout of love behind it. Through intervention the addict will understand the limits his dear ones have set and realize the fact that he has a problem and his family loves him in spite of it. More important, he will understand that the family will not continue putting up with his behavior. After all, relief of suffering, for both the addict and the family, is the primary agenda of any addiction intervention. Changing the self-destructive behavior at the source of suffering is always the focus regardless of the form a drug or alcohol intervention may take.

The wanted result of the intervention, obviously, is getting the alcoholic or drug abuser to agree that a problem exists and to ask for help. At this time, the interventionists are required to be equipped with enough knowledge on what treatment would be suitable for that particular person. The result of this intense research usually undermines the danger of the addict declining after treatment, causing greater difficulties and further risk, as well as continual pain and struggle for those around them.

2. To comprehend the variety and efficiency of different treatments and interventions that are meant to lessen the dependence on a substance. Advanced and highly effective treatment methods for drug and alcohol addiction are available in a wide range nowadays. A number of treatment and recovery program options can be considered for every patient. With a lot of choices, it would be advisable for those intervening on behalf of the abuser to agree on the program or method most suited to the addict. Ironically, the availability of so many options makes the selection of an appropriate treatment program a difficult task.

Everyone is biologically different, and reactions to alcohol/drug treatment can be different for each person. So the methods and time of treatment vary from patient to patient as the reaction varies according to the individual. Intervention, through which an expert determines the degree and nature of addiction, plays an important part in selecting an appropriate treatment program. In fact, the road map for the treatment program takes shape here.

The main goal of all treatment programs is getting addicts to achieve lasting restraint. However, a closer view reveals that there are more pressing goals, like reducing dependency on drugs so the patient will be capable of functioning. To get the maximum out of it, intervention needs to be conducted on a sane person. More important, the one who undergos intervention needs to remain sober throughout the entire process of intervention. In any case, attempting an intervention while a person is on a high will usually not be productive, because the addict cannot see many of their problems. So the treatment starts right with intervention.

The intervention team, after deciding on the treatment intended for the addict, is required to contact their chosen facility. The admittance procedure, financial obligation, and mode of treatment must be thoroughly discussed with the addict as well as the family. Addicts live and die on their chance to recover, so this is not a decision to be made on the spur of the moment.

3. To know more about treatment and intervention providers, effectual programs, and suitability of these treatments for that particular abuser. The addict needs to have a good idea of the alcohol/drug treatment programs he is supposed to undergo. Intervention, probably at a later stage, is the right time for giving him this information. Convincing the addict of the effect of the treatment is as important as making him recognize his addiction. Moreover, he can give valuable opinions while selecting an appropriate treatment program.

Basically, intervention is the step that comes before a person enters the recovering process. However, for many reasons, it can be considered the first and vital part of the treatment.

4. To boost community awareness of apt and successful treatment and other intervention programs for substance abuse. Intervention and treatment for alcohol and drug addiction are not at all one-on-one processes. Friends, family, colleagues, and even the employer of the addict have their part to play. Since the process is highly emotional and requires adequate support from everyone concerned, it is imperative that all have knowledge of the actual process, its goals, and its effects. An awareness of suitable and effective treatment will help them make good judgments of the behavior of people with drug dependency and to act in accordance with it.

People, including family and friends of the addict, often participate in the process of intervention with nervousness and sometimes frustration and anger. This may be because of their lack of knowledge, or because they are not fully convinced of the outcome and their need to put some effort into it. Since intervention is a collective effort in every respect, everyone who has a say in the process needs to be fully aware of it. Timely and well-planned intervention is essential for complete recovery from a drug addiction problem. The addiction intervention must be held with clear concern in a mild tone. To make the effort a success, it is important for all who participate in the intervention to be as clear with their goals as their intention.

III. PROCESS OF INTERVENTION

An addiction intervention is meant to be a calm, tender, realistic, relaxed dialogue. Seventy-five percent of interventions end up with addicts entering treatment that very day. Ninety-two percent of interventions end up with the addict in a rehab center within the week.

It is neither a confrontation nor a test of "who can be more pigheaded?" It is meant to better the lives, shrewdness, and choices of all involved. Even in our present day, people are still wary about what happens at an alcohol/drug intervention. In reality, it is very different from what actually takes place. Intervening for a person does not make one a "Judas." Standing up for a person and protecting him from himself does not make an interventionist a betrayer.

The most commonly used addiction interventional method is the ARISE method (A Relational Intervention Sequence for Engagement). Used in clinics all over the world, this three-point approach makes use of the level of effort used by the intervention network in relation to the addict's opposition to motivate him to start alcohol/drug treatment. Addiction intervention is all about forming a set of connective supports with the purpose of changing addictive behavior. With a trained professional helping, the members of the network facilitate each stage of the alcohol/drug intervention. Interventions are appropriate when the core members of the yet-to-be-formed support system can no longer just sit by in good conscience and watch the abuser decline. When they want to change the situation, the intervention can take place. As long as they feel there is a justifiable concern about the abuser's welfare (or their own), it is the perfect time to intervene. Time the substance abuse intervention when an alcoholic/addict is straight. Find a time when the addiction intervention team, as well as the abuser, is in a calm frame of mind.

ARISE Stages Include:

Stage I: Telephone interventions that motivate. By instilling hope and a positive mood that the alcohol/drug intervention will succeed, those who can and will help are invited to the intervention meeting. The group is organized and taught techniques to ensure the addict comes to the first meeting.

Stage II: Plan B, in case the addict fails to enter treatment even after the initial efforts. Face-to-face sessions are conducted with or without the addict present, to rally the support system in emergent motivational strategies, which have the primary goal of addiction treatment.

Stage III: This final limit-setting approach is not surprising to the addict and is an almost expected natural consequence. If the addiction intervention network has reached this point, the addict has been given and has rejected many chances to enter treatment. This means that he is aware that many of his loved ones are intervening for him.

Family members convey the limits they have set in a loving and supportive way. They too must learn to stop protecting the abuser from the consequences of their substance abuse and stop making apologies to others and getting them out of jams created by their behavior. Facing up to a few of the problems of their own making will make them fully experience the harmful effects of their habit. In fact, it is a form of reverse motivation. The ARISE process is intended to defend and augment the longevity of family relations, while at the same time eliminating the dependence and behavior from controlling the family.

The addiction intervention process, from initial inquiry to the actual meeting, can last several weeks to a day. In certain crises, however, immediate action must be taken to avert harm to the abuser as well as those around him. Analysis can in certain occasions come to paralysis; therefore, it is better to get out of the problem and into the solution as fast as possible. The healing process can begin only once intervention is over.

An addiction intervention team can consist of spiritual advisors, family, friends, or coworkers—together they make a well-rounded and effective team. However, if anyone coming to the intervention has "trust" issues, they can incapacitate the group effort, so it is important that the best possible team is chosen. When family secrets are revealed that may have contributed to the alcoholic's/addict's substance abuse, the "conspiracy of silence" is broken.

Unfortunately, it is the casual family or coworker interventions that can do more to estrange the abuser. This is because they find it difficult to distance themselves from the situation, and since emotions run high, there are opportunities to blame and provoke anger in both the alcoholic/addict and the interventionists, which merely complicates the situation. So a professional and detached addiction interventionist who brings in years of experience is often the best bet to avoid years of anxiety, outlay, and aggravation.

A professional interventionist can promptly organize the loved ones who want to help the addict into a focused support system while keeping in mind the main goal: the fastest way to alcohol/drug treatment and alcohol/drug rehab immediately. This MUST be done in a caring process that is transparent, confident, and optimistic, and with resolve. Most professional alcohol/drug interventions end with the addict safely in treatment. If this is not the case, the family, friends, and colleagues of the client must make the addict aware of all the consequences of his behavior. Strong and staunch limits must be set without any form of consideration to the addict's comfort. At the same time, the addict must understand that this is all done out of love for him. It must be apparent that this alcohol/drug abuse is not acceptable and that the family will not tolerate any situation where they are forced to be an audience to the addict's slow destruction of himself. Unless the addict is willing to help himself, the support system must ensure that no help, no support, no money, no sanctuary, not even a shoulder to lean on, nothing is extended until he requests treatment for substance abuse, whether alcohol or drugs. Intervention is a very excruciating process, because the true potency and doggedness of the addictive mind is then visible to the support system. Thus, a professional interventionist has to comfort and act as a buffer against all strong emotions to the abuser as well as his family.

Intervention is to be conducted in a serious, effective, safe, and confidential manner. It is a hands-on, enlightening process that concentrates on the unsettling bedlam and calamity within affected families. The intervention for alcohol/drug abuse is held in an effort to shift all people in the crisis, with the emphasis on the addict. Listen carefully to how the abuser is taking it. Answer and encourage him as he seeks help. Instead of answering concerns directly, support him and get him to call a professional for help. Act fast and get him into an addiction treatment program before he chickens out!

CONDUCTING AN INTERVENTION

It is important that those closest to the addict remember that the addict usually has a few traumatic events that occurred or are occurring due to his alcohol/drug abuse: he may lose his family or his closest friends. It is obvious to anyone why an addict must get into addiction treatment, but not as obvious to the addict himself. Therefore, the intervention team must identify significant problems that the addict faces and use them as leverage to prompt alcohol/drug rehab. Whether it is alcoholism or drug abuse, the addict needs to win over his addiction. Facing jail time, the imminent possibility of losing a spouse, or a comatose career are all possible situations that could pressure a person into fighting the addiction and seeking addiction treatment. The key here is to identify without a doubt what the addict holds dear to his heart and then use that to prod him into seeking treatment. An addict will only seek addiction intervention when something pushes him out of his comfort zone and into a decision for treatment.

Who Intervenes?

Who is present at the alcohol/drug intervention is of more importance than the number of people present. Most important is the person the addict most respects, and whose opinions are most highly regarded by him. It is this person whose support will be invaluable to the addict in getting rid of his alcohol/drug abuse. This is the person who would inform the abuser of the actual agenda. Once everyone agrees that the addict needs help and is supportive of the general agenda, all of them can be part of the addiction intervention team. It must be emphasized to the addict that his family cherishes him and that they all care for him. Short-tempered, antagonistic individuals who can't resist an argument should not be a part of the intervention team.

It is possible that the addict will definitely have put off or been scathing to most of the family at some time or other.

There is no doubt that he will have as many enemies within his family as without. However, arguments will not benefit or prompt the addict to seek addiction treatment. Instead, it merely stops the alcohol/drug intervention in its tracks as the focus shifts to the argument.

Though advisable, the presence of a professional substance abuse intervention counselor is not a necessity. The presence of pending legal issues, complete denial of any drug usage, external pressures—all such issues, which are extremely individual—must be intensely considered.

The addict must realize that his addiction is all out in the open and acknowledge that those involved in his intervention are there to ensure he gets treatment. Other problems and troubles must not sidetrack the main issue. The family must prepare to help the addict with his alcohol/drug abuse. People who intervene for the addict can be from within his family or can be anyone who has a loving, important relationship with the individual. All they have to do is strengthen and motivate the addict into alcohol/drug rehab. Embarrassing and mortifying the individual are not the best ways of achieving this.

When to Intervene?

The timing of an alcohol/drug intervention depends more on the events in the addict's life rather than on the family schedule. Your best opportunity to intervene for a loved one is just after a major event, such as when the abuser has been trapped in the aftereffects of his addiction. When caught in a crucial situation or when the addict shows signs of repentance or culpability would be the best time for an intervention. By postponing alcohol/drug intervention indefinitely, we are playing with the addict's life, and possibly the lives of others. Though it is more effective when the addict is suffering a particularly difficult backlash of his addiction, an addict's life cannot be risked by postponing an addiction intervention forever. Even in the absence of such trying situations, interventions can be successful if the family and addict are in close proximity so that the current state of affairs is known. A major roller coaster, the addict's life and its resultant problems cannot be hidden from close loved ones.

Another major consideration is the sobriety of the addict during intervention. Attempting any sort of intervention while the addict is on a high will usually not be productive, because the addict is unable to see his problems and will be inattentive.

Timely and well-planned intervention when the addict is unhinged provides the best opportunity for securing alcohol/drug rehab. The intervention must be held with clear concern and unwavering intention and tone. There is no need to commiserate with the addict, as empathy is a form of concurrence and may backfire by justifying the addiction.

How to Intervene?

Family members of the abuser are often more pitiable, because they are the ones who "enable" the abuser to behave every which way he pleases. In their denial of his alcohol/drug abuse, they tread softly around him, pretending they can't see what is happening under their very noses, all in the name of keeping peace in the home. By putting their collective foot down, the family has taken the first step in intervening for their loved one.

IV. Types of Treatment

Alcohol Intervention and Treatment

Alcoholics are often reluctant to accept the fact that they need assistance. Even if they recognize that they are out of control, they hate admitting it. Lack of confidence in therapies, reluctance to admit their own alcoholism, and the social problems associated with the addiction treatment are the main reasons for their negative behavior toward addiction intervention and treatment.

People often misread symptoms of alcoholism as character flaws. In fact, substance abuse is not a sign of moral weakness or lack of willpower. It is a treatable disorder, just like asthma or arthritis. Seeking help for alcoholism is not admitting some type of defect in oneself; it often takes great courage.

It is very important to get the alcoholic treatment as early as possible, and the more treatment given, the better the results. One cannot force an abuser to undergo treatment. He often cannot wait for things to get worse either. So, seeking the help of a professional addiction interventionist seems a feasible option to overcome alcohol abuse.

A professional interventionist can assess the crisis and determine the appropriateness of an alcohol intervention. After the clinical assessment of the addict's individual needs, an interventionist will suggest the most suitable treatment program and outline specific treatment options according to the specific needs of the alcoholic, such as location, clinical matters, and medical coverage. Through meetings and conversations, he will guide the alcoholic and others involved through the process of a professionally facilitated alcohol intervention.

Pre-intervention Meeting

During the pre-intervention meeting, the interventionist will talk about the alcohol abuse and its consequences in detail. He will discuss what the alcohol rehab program and recovery process will involve. There will also be the preparation and rehearsal of written statements to share with others who are involved in the alcoholism intervention process.

Intervention

The pre-intervention meeting is followed by the actual process of intervention. It is a prearranged, solution-focused process in which the family, close friends, and colleagues of the alcohol abuser are involved. They come together and present their observations and concerns regarding the alcoholic's behavior in a gentle and lenient manner.

Inpatient Care

For people with psychiatric disorders, delirium tremens, and those who have a troublesome home environment, alcoholism treatment performed in a hospital or in an alcohol treatment center is suitable. A patient who has undergone inpatient alcohol treatment seldom needs rehospitalization, and a longer abstinence is common among them. Inpatient alcohol abuse care is very comprehensive and includes many stages, such as a physical and psychiatric workup, detoxification, and medications. This type of alcohol treatment shows better success rates.

Outpatient Care

For people with moderate withdrawal symptoms, outpatient treatment is usually recommended. Family members and social support groups play a vital role in this type of alcohol rehab. Since alcoholism and smoking coexist in many people, quitting smoking can be helpful in promoting alcohol abstinence in outpatients and should be strongly encouraged.

An introduction to Alcoholics Anonymous (AA) or similar organizations is an important part of both inpatient and outpatient care.

Drug Therapy

Therapists use some drugs in the treatment of alcoholism. Antabuse (disulfiram) is a widely used one that has been available for many years. This drug, which does not have any effect on the craving to drink, causes an unbearable sickness when alcohol is consumed. Alcoholics, knowing that they will get sick if they drink, will definitely try to stay sober. But the effect of this drug is for a limited period only. Alcoholics can start drinking again after a certain period of time. Medications such as Revia (naltrexone) and acamprosate lessen the craving for alcohol and the pleasing effects of alcohol consumption.

Cognitive-Behavioral Therapy (CBT)

Cognitive-behavioral therapy (CBT) is recommended for people with severe alcoholism. CBT uses a structured teaching approach that includes instructions and homework given to improve patients' ability to deal with everyday life and to change the way they think about drinking. A combination of CBT and opioid antagonists is particularly effective.

Drug Intervention and Treatment

Problems associated with a person's drug addiction may vary considerably with the patient's mental health, physical health, social problems, and background. These factors may complicate treatment. Selection of an appropriate substance abuse treatment program, which plays an important role in achieving the ultimate goal of lasting abstinence, is an important step. Severity of addiction, financial background, need for other medical treatment, and the physical condition of the addict are the factors considered in determining the type of treatment program. Depending on the needs of the patient, the treatment may be short-term or long-term.

The symptoms of chemical dependency and psychiatric illness are similar. This makes diagnosis and treatment more difficult. As both disorders are often seen together, their symptoms may overlap and even disguise each other.

Maintenance Treatment Method

In this treatment the patient is required to switch over to a similar drug that produces milder withdrawal symptoms. For example, in the treatment for heroin addicts, patients are given an oral dose of a synthetic opiate, usually methadone hydrochloride, at a dosage sufficient to block the effects of heroin. Methadone suppresses narcotic withdrawal for twenty-four to thirty-six hours. The patient can disengage from drug-seeking and related criminal behavior at this stage. Though the patient remains physically dependent on the opioid, the uncontrolled and disruptive behavior seen in heroin addicts can be avoided.

Outpatient Drug-Free Treatment

This medication-free program requires regular visits to a clinic. In fact, it covers a wide variety of programs for different patients. Individual or group counseling is the main part of this program. This treatment is commonly recommended for patients with only brief histories of drug dependence.

Therapeutic Communities (TCs)

These are highly structured residence programs that last for six to twelve months. This method is effective on patients with long histories of drug dependence, involvement in criminal activities, and badly damaged social functioning. The clean and sober atmosphere that TCs provide is the most significant feature of this program. Moreover, these programs provide patients the opportunity to associate with people who share the same goal. They become a part of the community they live in and assume more and more responsibility with the progress of time. Studies show that those who successfully complete residential treatment have lower levels of drug use, criminal behavior, and depression in comparison with those who undergo other treatment methods.

Short-term residential programs based on the Minnesota Model of treatment for alcoholism involve three to six weeks of inpatient treatment followed by outpatient treatment or participation in Narcotics Anonymous or Cocaine Anonymous.

Supplementary Treatment Programs

Many treatment approaches developed and supported by the National Institute on Drug Abuse (NIDA) are widely used to supplement existing treatment programs for drug addiction. Some of these are listed below.

Supportive-expressive psychotherapy is used for the treatment of heroin and cocaine addicts. This therapy uses techniques to help patients say their piece and feel relaxed in
discussing their personal experiences. Supportive-expressive
psychotherapy, in combination with drug counseling, is being
effectively used for the treatment of opiate addicts with psychiatric problems.

Relapse prevention, a cognitive-behavioral therapy origi-
nally developed for the treatment of problem drinking and
modified later for cocaine addicts, encompasses many cognitive-
behavioral approaches that facilitate abstinence. This is particularly effective on people who experience relapse. This treatment helps patients develop coping strategies for problems
they are likely to encounter. Skills patients acquire during this
therapy remain and can be used in improving their lives even
after the completion of the treatment.

Individualized drug counseling, which focuses directly on
stopping the addict's illegal drug use and deals with related
areas such as employment status and family or social relations,
helps the patient develop coping tactics and tools for abstain-
ing from drug use.

Motivational enhancement therapy is intended to initiate a
behavior change. It resolves the confusion about engaging in
treatment and stopping drug use. This treatment consists of an
initial session and three to four individual treatment sessions
with a therapist. The first session provides feedback generated
from the initial assessment, and in the following sessions, the
counselor observes changes and reviews ending strategies that
are being used. This therapy has proved successful among
marijuana abusers.

Aftercare counseling. Recovering addicts need to attend aftercare counseling to overcome the uncertainties and anxiety they have when they resume living in a regular environment. They often grow nervous in normal surroundings. Aftercare programs normally last for six months to a year. They equip an addict with tools that are required to complete recovery. Recovering addicts should attend Narcotics Anonymous meetings during this period. The aftercare program should be tailored to serve the needs of the person and cover all areas such as lifestyle changes, educational and career guidance, financial planning, and self-progress.

Appendix 5B: Additional Resources

Alcoholics Anonymous World Services, Inc.
(212) 870-3400
P.O. Box 459
New York, NY 10163
www.alcoholics-anonymous.org

Al-Anon Family Group Headquarters, Inc.
800-356-9996
800-356-2666
1600 Corporate Landing Parkway
Virginia Beach, VA 23457-5617
www.alanon.alateen.org

Cocaine Anonymous
6125 Washington Boulevard, Suite 202
Los Angeles, CA 90230

Columbia Addiction and Substance Abuse Center (CASA)
www.casacollumbia.org

DrinkWise
800-272-5145
P.O. Box 435
Ann Arbor, MI 48106
www.med.umich.edu/drink-wise

Marijuana Anonymous
P.O. Box 2912
Van Nuys, CA 91404

Moderation Management
(612) 512-1484

Narcotics Anonymous
818-773-9999
P.O. Box 9999
Van Nuys, CA 91409

National Center on Addiction and Substance Abuse
152 West 57th Street
New York, NY 10019

National Clearinghouse for Alcohol and Drug Information
800-729-6686
P.O. Box 2345
Rockville, MD 20847-2345

Appendix 6: The Twelve Steps of Alcoholics Anonymous*

1. We admitted we were powerless over alcohol—that our lives had become unmanageable.

2. Came to believe that a Power greater than ourselves could restore us to sanity.

3. Made a decision to turn our will and our lives over to the care of God as we understood Him.

4. Made a searching and fearless moral inventory of ourselves.

5. Admitted to God, to ourselves, and to another human being the exact nature of our wrongs.

6. Were entirely ready to have God remove all these defects of character.

7. Humbly asked Him to remove our shortcomings.

8. Made a list of all persons we had harmed and became willing to make amends to them all.

---

*Reprinted by permission of Alcoholics Anonymous World Service, Inc. Permission to reprint this material does not imply that AA has reviewed or approved the contents of this publication, nor that AA agrees with the views expressed herein.

9. Made direct amends to such people wherever possible, except when to do so would injure them or others.

10. Continued to take personal inventory, and when we were wrong promptly admitted it.

11. Sought through prayer and meditation to improve our conscious contact with God, as we understood Him, praying only for knowledge of His will for us and the power to carry that out.

12. Having had a spiritual awakening as a result of these steps, we tried to carry that message to alcoholics, and to practice these principles in all our affairs.

Appendix 7:
Topics and Questions for Discussion

1. After his twin brother died, Scott experienced excruciating bodily pain. "Each doctor who examined me, probed me, or cut into me hoped to be the one to reveal the source of my pain. But one by one, they failed, and gave me painkillers as a consolation prize. Somehow, though, I knew that this unremitting pain lay far deeper than any knife or endoscope could reach. . . . Jonathan's death had created a cavernous void inside of me that could not simply be filled." Do you have an example in your own life of when emotional pain manifested as physical pain? Or a time when your body sent you signals about stress or anxiety in the form of bodily pain?

2. The afterword explains that "Our hearts, minds, and souls show us how to lead what has been called an 'authentic' life. Living authentically is not a guarantee of happiness." Do you agree or disagree with this? Do you have an example of a time when you were not living authentically and when you felt off-kilter because of it? What did you do?

3. Everyone experiences the stages of grief differently. Have you ever been stuck in a stage of grief (shock, anger, denial, bargaining, acceptance)? How did you move

beyond it? What aspects of Scott's grief can you relate to?

4. In the beginning of the book, Scott and his brother were bar mitzvahed, and later in the book, Scott mentions that he has been baptized into the Christian faith. How do you think faith can help someone through the grieving process? Has it ever helped you? How?

5. As an identical twin, Scott was blessed with a unique relationship with his brother—he literally felt what his brother felt. Whether you are a twin or not, have you ever experienced a close psychic bond with a sibling or someone close to you? How?

6. In Chapter 5, Scott is told that no one is to know about Jonathan's illness. "It will be Jonathan's decision when he decides to tell the family," his mother said. Do you think that if there were no "family" expectations it would have been easier for Jonathan to reveal his secret? Do you have examples of family secrets?

7. As Scott is trying to avoid grieving the loss of his brother, he has repeated dreams in which his brother appears. Have you ever in your life had a repeated dream? If so, what was it, and what do you think it meant? Did any of your dreams stop occurring in a significant way when you had resolved the problem or moved on in your life?

8. In the beginning of the book, the author describes an idyllic childhood with typical boyhood adventures. "As our mother knew, the creek was indeed dangerous; it had a very tall concrete culvert that spanned over it, creating an immense and dark channel that the creek

drained into. The edge of the culvert sloped downward and could easily send a young child tumbling twenty feet into the creek below. Mom had warned Jonathan and me of the danger many times, but of course, that only made it seem more mysterious and appealing." In your own childhood, did you have an infamous "creek," and did you go anyway? What happened?

9. In Chapter 19, Scott reveals that "In death, he was teaching me how to live." Do you have any examples of this in your own life?

10. In Chapter 20, Scott's sponsor, Hank, explains the meaning of finding Jonathan's poetry: "I think he wants you to know him better now than you ever did when he was alive. I think what you found was his gift to you." Have you ever had an experience when you knew someone more intimately or in a deeper or truer way after they had died?

11. Allston the cat, Jon's cherished companion, appears many times during the book. Have you ever cared for a pet after the death of its owner? How can pets be affected by the death of their owner? Has a pet ever helped you grieve?

12. In the book, Scott reveals the anger and frustration his wife displayed as he continued to use drugs. Have you had a similar experience where you continued to do something that was unacceptable to your significant other/partner? How did she/he feel? How did you both resolve this?

13. The author describes a paranormal experience where he
felt Jonathan's presence. "Many times lying in bed at
night I could feel a presence in my room, as though
someone were watching me. The sensation was strange,
the room dark and empty, with an aura around me that
made me feel as if I were not alone. One night when I
was watching television, I restlessly changed the channels with the remote, and the name 'Jonathan' was
broadcast from every channel. While one mention of his
name would have seemed merely a coincidence, I heard
his name spoken on several different channels, one after
another. I didn't know if this was my mind playing tricks
on me or truly some paranormal presence of Jonathan."
Do you believe in after-death communication? Have you
ever experienced it?

About the Author

*S*cott M. Davis, M.D., is an internist and addiction medicine specialist. After graduating from Boston University School of Medicine, he completed his medical training in Internal Medicine at the University of California, and subsequently, through a fellowship in Addiction Medicine with Loma Linda University School of Medicine. Dr. Davis is currently the only full-time addiction medicine physician for the world-renowned Betty Ford Center in Rancho Mirage, California. He also serves as a clinical instructor in the treatment of chemical dependency on the faculty of Loma Linda University School of Medicine.

Dr. Davis is recognized by the American Society of Addiction Medicine as a national mentor for addiction treatment and is regarded as a leading expert in the field of addiction medicine. He has been published in numerous periodicals and newspapers, including the *Journal of Addictive Diseases,* the *American Journal of Cardiology,* and *Men's Health* magazine.

Dr. Davis lives in Palm Desert, California, with his wife, Rebecca, and their two daughters.